# War and Health

# War and Health: Lessons from the Gulf War

Edited by

**Professor Harry Lee**
*Former Head of Gulf War Veterans Medical Assessment
Programme at St. Thomas' Hospital, London, UK*

and

**Professor Edgar Jones**
*King's Centre for Military Health Research, London, UK*

John Wiley & Sons, Ltd

Copyright © 2007    John Wiley & Sons Ltd, The Atrium, Southern Gate, Chichester,
West Sussex PO19 8SQ, England

Telephone    (+44) 1243 779777

Email (for orders and customer service enquiries): cs-books@wiley.co.uk
Visit our Home Page on www.wiley.com

*Other Wiley Editorial Offices*

John Wiley & Sons Inc., 111 River Street, Hoboken, NJ 07030, USA

Jossey-Bass, 989 Market Street, San Francisco, CA 94103-1741, USA

Wiley-VCH Verlag GmbH, Boschstr. 12, D-69469 Weinheim, Germany

John Wiley & Sons Australia Ltd, 33 Park Road, Milton, Queensland 4064, Australia

John Wiley & Sons (Asia) Pte Ltd, 2 Clementi Loop #02-01, Jin Xing Distripark, Singapore 129809

John Wiley & Sons Canada Ltd, 6045 Freemont Blvd, Mississauga, Ontario, L5R 4J3, Canada

Wiley also publishes its books in a variety of electronic formats. Some content that appears in print
may not be available in electronic books.

Anniversary Logo Design: Richard J. Pacifico

*Library of Congress Cataloging in Publication Data*

War and health : lessons from the Gulf War / edited by Harry Lee and Edgar Jones.
    p.   ;   cm.
Includes bibliographical references and index.
ISBN 978-0-470-51229-6 (alk. paper)
1. Persian Gulf syndrome. 2. Post–traumatic stress disorder. 3. Veterans—Mental health.
4. Persian Gulf War, 1991—Psychological aspects. 5. Persian Gulf War, 1991—Health aspects.
6. Persian Gulf War, 1991—Veterans—Diseases. I. Lee, H. A. (Harry André) II. Jones,
Edgar, 1953–
[DNLM: 1. Persian Gulf Syndrome—psychology. 2. Combat Disorders. 3. Gulf War.
4. Persian Gulf Syndrome—etiology. 5. Stress Disorders, Post–Traumatic. 6. Veterans—
psychology. WM 184 W253 2007]
RC552.P67W3775 2007
616.85′212—dc22

                                                  2007010093

*British Library Cataloguing in Publication Data*

A catalogue record for this book is available from the British Library

ISBN 978-0-470-51229-6

Typeset in 10.5/13pt Sabon by Integra Software Services Pvt. Ltd, Pondicherry, India
Printed and bound in Great Britain by T.J. International Ltd, Padstow, Cornwall.
This book is printed on acid-free paper responsibly manufactured from sustainable forestry
in which at least two trees are planted for each one used for paper production.

# Contents

# List of Contributors

Keron Fletcher
Combat Stress
Audley Avenue
Newport
Shropshire TF10 7DR
UK

Edgar Jones
Institute of Psychiatry and King's Centre for Military Health Research
Weston Education Centre
10 Cutcombe Road
London SE5 9RJ
UK

Susie Kilshaw
Department of Anthropology
University College London
Gower Street
London WC1E 6BT
UK

Harry Lee
Former Head of Gulf War Veterans Medical Assessment Programme at
St Thomas's Hospital,
London
UK

# Foreword

Gulf War health issues have reached an important juncture. Millions have been spent on research into numerous controversies surrounding what befell veterans of this conflict. The best work has already been completed and further studies are unlikely to add much to our current body of knowledge. Clinics set up to evaluate the health of these veterans are closing down and physicians are moving on to other endeavours. Most veterans have left the military and have started careers in the civilian world. They are being looked after by health care providers whose knowledge of what transpired has been heavily influenced by what they have seen and heard in the media, a notoriously unreliable source of information. There is a need for a practical source of authoritative information easily accessible and understood by those now caring for our veterans. This book meets that need.

A publication of this nature would be incomplete without an exploration of historical precedents. Understanding what we are dealing with now is immeasurably aided by looking at what has transpired in the past. This is a fascinating exercise with insights gleaned that seem obvious on reflection but that are not intuitively evident at first. Similar problems have been well documented amongst veterans of conflicts going back almost two centuries. There are tantalizing hints of evidence supportive of this fact reaching even further into our distant past. The problems that have emerged, however, have not been identical. There is no single 'syndrome' that maps onto every conflict. Professor Jones is arguably the world's most prolific publisher of articles on puzzling maladies that have gripped soldiers of numerous past battles. He has a wealth of information on factors that may have influenced their development and he is an easy read.

How best to explain what has negatively influenced the quality of life of veterans of the first Gulf War? The first and most obvious explanation that comes to mind is that these veterans must have sustained an environmental exposure while deployed that has damaged them in a permanent way. Similar hypotheses were raised in other historical conflicts. Numerous expert medical and scientific panels have reviewed the evidence for harm from environmental exposures sustained during the Gulf War and have found this evidence wanting. Indeed, this would not be surprising. The environmental exposures of historical concern have rarely been the same. Importantly, we know that similar health concerns at an identical prevalence have arisen in members of a Gulf War unit that were rotated home before the conflict even began. Veterans of this unit were not exposed to any of the environmental factors that have been raised as possibly being relevant yet they are still unwell. Importantly too, we know that similar health complaints have arisen in conflicts that took place after the Gulf War, including those in Croatia, Cambodia and the Balkans. Exposures were different for each.

Professor Lee is one of those rare individuals who have been afforded the opportunity to examine a large number of Gulf War veterans over a long period of time. He is in an ideal situation to address causation of illnesses and clinical outcomes of investigations. Civilian clinicians who may have only one or two veterans in their practice are now caring for most Gulf War veterans. Professor Lee has carefully recorded insights and observations on this issue that will be invaluable to doctors now responsible for these veterans. Such a reference source has not been readily available to these health care providers. This book will allow these providers to answer questions from their patients in an informed manner. This is all most veterans are asking. Professor Lee tackles the difficult issue of 'Gulf War syndrome' and concludes that the evidence available does not support the emergence of a new medical diagnosis. The vast majority of clinicians who have had the most experience examining these patients support this conclusion. Gulf War veterans certainly have more symptoms than their non-Gulf war veteran military colleagues. More symptoms are not the same as more diagnoses. The Gulf War was a very significant event in the lives of these veterans and they have come home changed, both from their own perspective and from the perspective of their loved ones. For many, their quality of life is not the same. Professor Lee has much to share that will help physicians help these veterans.

If we are ever to intervene in an effective way to mitigate or prevent future illnesses arising after conflicts, we have to improve our understanding of the dynamics involved in the development of belief systems themselves. Most adults depend on the media, the Internet and their network of friends to inform themselves of what is happening in the world around them. Sir William Osler, the father of internal medicine, noted over one hundred years ago that 'If you read something in a newspaper that you know to be true . . . begin to doubt it at once.' The

Internet is an even more unreliable source of accurate information for most sites visited. We trust friends and acquaintances more readily than we trust most authority figures. Medical anthropology is a discipline that can shed light on how our oral narratives can be constructed to help us make sense of this complex world we live in. It can also explain how things can sometimes go wrong. Susie Kilshaw, as a medical anthropologist with a particular interest in 'Gulf War syndrome', is in a unique position to inform us in this important area of study.

At the end of the day, veterans want to know what can be done for them and where they can access this help. Keron Fletcher has provided a useful guide for medical practitioners to the various services available to this veteran population. He explores the history, the theories and the practical approaches to mental health issues that have arisen after conflicts. He provides practical real-life examples to illustrate the points he is making. He comes at this from the perspective of a professional actually involved with seeing and addressing the difficult and complex mental health problems that can occur in veteran populations. This real-life experience is a strength of this chapter.

Healthcare providers need an accurate source of practical information to assist them in caring for Gulf War veterans. It is easy to ask even the most basic of questions concerning health outcomes of Gulf War veterans and find disappointing misinformation in the possession of veterans, the public at large, journalists and politicians. Experienced professionals, intimately familiar with the facts, have authored this book. It fills the information void that most civilian physicians encounter about this issue. The timing of this publication could not be more opportune, as most Gulf War assessment clinics have shut down and veterans have transitioned into the civilian world. This publication would not have been possible without the cooperation of veterans and their families from multiple countries who have made themselves available for clinical evaluations and for participation in research projects. This book is a distillation of all the important things that have been learned from them. It is a valuable tool for those health care providers who continue to be involved with this interesting population.

Ken Scott
Canada

# 1

# Introduction

## Harry Lee and Edgar Jones

Standard medical texts give scant, if any, coverage, to the assessment and treatment of veterans who experience difficulties in managing the transition from the high-intensity demands of battle to those of civilian life. The *Oxford Textbook of Medicine*, for example, has no entries on so-called 'Gulf War syndrome' (Warrell *et al.*, 2005). The two-volume *Oxford Textbook of Psychiatry* includes a short section on Da Costa's syndrome, or disordered action of the heart, but has no entries on recent post-combat disorders (Gelder *et al.*, 1986). Although a bewildering variety of papers has been published in specialist medical journals on the theme of Gulf-related illness, until recently no consensus had emerged about the true nature of these health concerns, their causes and what, indeed, should be done to address them. Such is the complexity and breadth of these publications, which range from neurology, rheumatology, immunology, reproductive medicine and anthropology through to psychiatry, that the general practitioner or medical student may find it difficult, if not impossible, to reach a balanced judgement about the status of so-called 'Gulf War syndrome' without extensive study. In March 2006, a special edition of the *Philosophical Transactions of the Royal Society* sought to summarise the state of knowledge for all the medical disciplines involved (Wessely and Freedman, 2006). This book is designed to serve as a practical adjunct to these scientific papers, relating their findings to what is seen in clinics and outpatient departments.

*War and Health: Lessons from the Gulf War*   Edited by Harry Lee & Edgar Jones
© 2007 John Wiley & Sons, Ltd

Iraq invaded Kuwait on 2nd August 1990. Shortly afterwards, Coalition forces, led by the United States, began a military deployment known as Operation Desert Shield. On 15th/16th January 1991 an air campaign against Iraq began, followed on 24th February by a ground war that lasted for only four days. Iraqi forces were defeated and driven from Kuwait; the assault on their army in retreat down the Basra road offered many of the most graphic images of the conflict. The main component of the Coalition forces was provided by the United States with 697 000 personnel. The United Kingdom also made a substantial contribution with over 53 000 troops, while other Coalition members included Saudi Arabia, Egypt, Oman, France, Syria, Kuwait, Pakistan, Canada, Bahrain, Morocco and Qatar.

Shortly (1992/3) after the cessation of hostilities, reports began to emerge in the US of clusters of unusual illnesses occurring amongst Gulf War veterans. Claims were made that previously fit veterans had developed unusual diseases and symptoms. Stories were also told of children with birth defects being born to the wives of Gulf War veterans. These frightening accounts rapidly attracted the attention of the media and veterans' pressure groups. Soon, long stories circulated about cover-ups and government conspiracies.

This book is based on the premise that health-care professionals who treat veterans require an understanding of military culture, syndromes characterised by medically unexplained symptoms, and post-trauma psychiatric illness, including post-traumatic stress disorder (PTSD). Service life and, in particular, the demands of combat have little in common with daily civilian existence. The difficulties that veterans encounter in trying to come to terms with their experiences of war and the adjustment to a routine peace-time existence require a measure of specific inside knowledge.

Armed forces are hierarchical social groupings. In battle the immediate interests of the individual are suppressed to enhance the value of the unit to which they belong. Group dynamics are well understood in terms of training and motivation to undertake hazardous tasks. However, when soldiers leave the army, they are excluded from their units and often find themselves feeling isolated. In the past, comrades associations, such as the Royal British Legion, have helped to manage the transition to civilian life. For those ex-servicemen who feel disaffected and let down by the military, these semi-official bodies are sometimes not attractive. Some have joined pressure groups as a way of dealing with their discontents and health issues.

During the First World War, 5.7 million men joined the UK armed forces and virtually every male doctor who qualified at the time of the conflict volunteered for military service. A similar situation existed during the Second World War when, through air raids, rationing and the threat of invasion, the conflict was spread through much of the civilian population. In the post-1945 period, National Service recruited a wide cross-section of British society. With the end of National Service in 1960 and progressive defence cuts, the 'military footprint', or those individuals with direct knowledge of the armed forces, has receded. Regular service personnel currently number 196 650, divided between 108 150 in the army, 39 390 in the Royal Navy and 49 120 in the Royal Air Force. Today, few GPs or hospital consultants have served in the military. Indeed, the forces medical services are under strength and in time of conflict rely on the Territorial Army to supplement their numbers in theatre.

Despite the continued reduction in the size of our armed forces, military issues remain high profile. Wars, veterans and, increasingly, psychological trauma attract the attention of journalists and form the subject of press reports and public inquiries. Hence, as disseminated knowledge about veterans' health has declined throughout society, it has become a focus of interest and speculation. The debate around the nature of 'Gulf War syndrome' became polarized between relatively small numbers of scientists and doctors who study the health of soldiers, and suspicious media and increasingly vociferous ex-servicemen's pressure groups. As a result, veterans' health has become politicised and subject to a number of institutional and semi-official inquiries. Although those set up by the Medical Research Council in the UK and the Institute of Medicine in the US reached a broad agreement, the recent, so-called, 'independent' investigation by Lord Lloyd disagreed with their findings and called for further studies based purely on a scientistic approach.

With contributors drawn from a variety of backgrounds, this multi-disciplinary book is designed to offer health-care professionals an insight into the physical, mental and social problems experienced by veterans returning to civilian life. Although most servicemen make the adjustment successfully and find fulfilling roles as citizens, others struggle to achieve the status and satisfaction they enjoyed when in uniform. By examining the problems experienced by veterans of the Gulf War, it may provide lessons of value to the current and future conflicts.

# REFERENCES

Gelder, M., Gath, D., and Mayou, R. (1986). *Oxford Textbook of Psychiatry*, Oxford: Oxford University Press.

Warrell, D.A., Cox, T.M., Firth, J.D. and Benz, J.D. (2005). *Oxford Textbook of Medicine*, Oxford: Oxford University Press.

Wessely, S. and Freedman, L. (2006). Reflections on Gulf War illness, *Philosophical Transactions of the Royal Society*, **361**, 531–32.

# 2

# Post-combat Disorders:
# the Boer War to the Gulf

Edgar Jones

Even a cursory examination of military history will show that modern wars have produced a bewildering variety of post-combat disorders. On the surface, these appear to have little in common with each other: not only do their labels suggest diversity (including wind contusion, soldier's heart, debility, heatstroke, shellshock, neurasthenia, effort syndrome, gas hysteria, non-ulcer dyspepsia, effects of Agent Orange and Gulf War syndrome), but the symptoms and explanations tied to these diagnoses suggest disparate aetiologies and pathological mechanisms. Among the causes proposed have been toxic exposures (to poisonous gases, organophosphates depleted uranium, dioxin, a defoliant), the after-effects of disease (dysentery, enteric fever and bacterial infection), unhealthy diet, side effects of vaccinations, and even badly designed equipment.

In an attempt to clarify the status of so-called 'Gulf War syndrome', Hyams *et al.* (1996) argued on the basis of symptoms, that post-combat disorders had much in common and could be sub-divided into two groups: those that had a psychological explanation (neurasthenia, shell-shock, battle exhaustion, combat fatigue and PTSD) and those for which a physical cause was identified (irritable heart, Da Costa's syndrome, effort syndrome, effects of Agent Orange and Gulf War syndrome). Based on contemporary reports by both doctors and patients, they not

*War and Health: Lessons from the Gulf War*   Edited by Harry Lee & Edgar Jones
© 2007 John Wiley & Sons, Ltd

only identified common symptoms but also 'a second possible unifying factor', namely the high frequency of reported diarrhoea and other infectious diseases preceding the onset of such syndromes. However, Hyams *et al.* concluded that 'no unique war-related disease is evident' (1996, p. 403).

## HISTORICAL PRESENTATIONS

### US Civil War

The first war in which post-combat disorders presented a serious medical problem was probably the American Civil War (1861–64), when troops on both sides were diagnosed with soldier's heart, irritable heart and nostalgia. Many Northern soldiers found themselves referred to the US Army Hospital for Injuries and Diseases of the Nervous System, Turner's Lane, Philadelphia. There, Jacob Da Costa (1833–1900), a physician who had studied internal medicine in Paris, Prague and Vienna, conducted research into the cause of their puzzling symptoms (Wooley, 1982; Wooley, 2002). Da Costa discovered that 39 % of such patients had been subject to 'hard field service and excessive marching', while a further 31 % had previously suffered from diarrhoea (Da Costa, 1871, p. 37; Dean, 1997). A popular explanation proposed in both America and the UK was that the webbing designed to support the soldier's knapsack and other equipment pressed heavily on the chest. This pressure, in turn, constricted the arteries serving both the heart and lungs, leading to palpitations and breathing difficulties (Maclean, 1864). In some cases the heart appeared to have been irreversibly damaged and significant numbers of servicemen were invalided from the British Army, often with a permanent war pension

By 1871, Da Costa had rejected this explanation. Since 'irritable heart' was not confined to the infantry but affected the cavalry and artillery, he argued that the webbing and packs, which varied between these arms, could not have been the primary cause. Although this was widely regarded as a disorder limited to soldiers, Da Costa had observed that the clinical presentation in troops could be duplicated in civilians 'from the experience of private practice' (Da Costa, 1871, p. 17). Having identified 15 cases that showed signs of cardiac atrophy (Oppenheimer, 1942), he concluded that disordered action in the long term could lead to organic disease, though subsequent research by others failed to confirm his hypothesis.

A victorious Unionist administration, wishing to compensate the servicemen who had endured such difficult conditions during the Civil War, granted pensions to those who had been disabled. The number of ex-servicemen receiving a pension rose from 123 000 in 1875 to a peak of 419 000 in 1891. Although initially modest, public opinion led later administrations to introduce regular increments, which in turn increased the total expenditure to almost $250 million by 1921 (Clark, 1931, p. 196). By the 1920s these pensions had become sufficiently generous for it to be said that attractive young women patrolled the public parks of New York near the homes of elderly veterans. They offered marriage knowing that this would be brief, while they would continue to receive a handsome reward for the remainder of their lives (Sargant, 1967). Lawsuits and appeals were common in the aftermath of the Civil War, as servicemen attempted to establish a claim for a pension.

## South Africa

For the British Army, the Boer War (1899–1902) was the first time that post-combat disorders became a prominent matter of medical concern. Although soldiers had been invalided from India with similar clusters of symptoms throughout the latter part of the Nineteenth century, these had usually been explained as the effects of extreme heat. In South Africa the increase in their incidence and a comparatively benign climate, troubled the authorities. Rheumatism and disordered action of the heart (DAH) were the main diagnoses attached to medically unexplained symptoms (Jones and Wessely, 2001). DAH was the term adopted by British military doctors in the late 1880s to replace palpitation or soldier's heart. It was characterised by the presence of murmurs, irregular heartbeat, shortness of breath, chest pain, and general feelings of weakness and fatigue. Because investigative techniques were limited to auscultation and percussion, together with post-mortem studies, cardiologists tended to conceptualise heart disease in terms of morbid anatomy, such as deformity of the valves (Cantor, 2000). As a result, they struggled to understand disturbances of function, often failing to distinguish between serious disease and non-organic abnormalities. In acute febrile illness, for example, the hyperdynamic circulation can produce a systolic murmur, which in the late Nineteenth century was sometimes misinterpreted as a sign of an organic lesion. Because 'simple continued fever' (SCF) was a common diagnosis for troops serving in South Africa, many found themselves labelled as suffering from the potentially more serious VDH.

Between 1902 and 1911, the number of discharges from the British Army for DAH rose fourfold (Anon, 1912). However, an investigation by the professor of tropical medicine at the Royal Army Medical College revealed that most of the increase could be explained by the effects of the Boer War, and that there had been a modest fall in the rate from 1908 to 1910, which was attributed to the introduction of the new methods of physical training. Although physicians did not usually confirm such cases as organic heart disease, they remained uncertain about its aetiology and, erring on the side of caution, recommended a sedentary lifestyle. In addition, equally large numbers of soldiers were discharged with so-called valvular disease of the heart (VDH). Although there were small numbers of serious cardiac disease, follow-up studies involving death certificates have shown that the majority were misdiagnosed functional disorders (Jones *et al.*, 2003a). Because veterans with DAH or VDH were discouraged from undertaking heavy manual work, and thus denied a widespread source of income, they were entitled to apply for a pension from the Royal Hospital, Chelsea (Dean, 1950).

## World War One

The first post-combat disorder to attract the attention of the general public arose in World War One. Indeed, shellshock, a term that has never been properly defined, is still used today to describe a person upset by a traumatic event. The adoption of the label by the press, military doctors, soldiers themselves, politicians and the literary fraternity from 1915 onwards, demonstrated that it had finally been acknowledged that war could exercise a powerful effect on a soldier's mind (Shephard, 1996). It was crucially related to the nature of trench warfare (see below). Nevertheless, there was a significant difference between today's concept of psychological trauma and that prevalent during World War One. The idea that a soldier could suffer 'psychical' effects without a demonstrable physical wound was combined with traditional notions of heredity. In the pre-1914 period, mental illness was considered a product of either a diseased constitution or the effects of degeneration as it spread through growing industrial conurbations. Although it was acknowledged that some recruits were particularly vulnerable to the stress of warfare and should be filtered at enlistment, most cases of shellshock were thought preventable. Under the chairmanship of Lord Southborough, the War Office Committee into the effects of shellshock, which reported in 1922, concluded that this disorder could be eliminated by screening, training, good leadership and *esprit de corps* (Southborough, 1922).

Shellshock was not the only post-combat disorder of World War One, as examples of DAH and VDH were just as numerous. A new range of causal explanations was proposed, building on the hypotheses advanced during the Boer War. The trenches of World War One were insanitary and trench fever was commonplace. Sir James Mackenzie argued, from a survey of over 2000 soldiers with DAH, that in 80 % of cases the 'first onset of their illness began with some complaint of an infectious nature, such as measles, influenza, trench fever, typhoid fever, malaria, dysentery or PUO' (Mackenzie, 1920, p. 534). Having found that 32 % of 558 patients with DAH had suffered from an infectious disease immediately before the onset of cardiac symptoms, Thomas Lewis concluded that this was 'the dominant etiological factor' (Lewis, 1918, p. 33). In addition, he discovered that 63 cases (11 %) had been precipitated by wounds, bombardment, gassing or frostbite. Furthermore, Venning analysed 7803 DAH and VDH cases admitted to No. 1 Convalescent Depot between November 1916 and November 1918 (Venning, 1919, pp. 337–38). He found that infection was the precipitating factor in 21.5 % of cases – of which rheumatic fever was the most common complaint (50.3 %) followed by PUO (16.3 %). Interestingly, Venning proposed that the 'physical and mental strain' of active service was a significant cause accounting for 28.2% of cases, adding (Venning, 1919, p. 338):

'It was impossible in many cases to distinguish whether the strain was mental or physical, the symptoms produced being identical... The effects of this were clearly shown by the large number of admissions after the German push towards Amiens in March and April 1918'.

Between 1880 and the 1930, the observation that neurasthenia frequently followed infection was widely held. For most physicians, including Osler, Oppenheim, Cobb, Horder and others, the principle candidate was influenza, but claims were also made for various alimentary bacteria, typhoid, and even the effects of vaccination (Wessely, 1991, p. 927).

## World War Two

Although use of the term 'shellshock' was proscribed by the military and medical authorities in July 1939, in an attempt to prevent a flood of war pension claims (Shephard, 1999), this action did not prevent the emergence of other post-combat disorders during World War Two. Prominent among the referrals to general hospitals were cases of non-ulcer dyspepsia or suspected duodenal ulcer (Tidy, 1941, 1943). Having only limited and unreliable instruments of detection (the fractional meal test, which involved withdrawing samples of gastric juices through a Ryle's tube at regular intervals to assess acidity levels, occult bloods and the barium meal), both physicians and radiologists understandably practiced defensive medicine. When confronted with ambiguous evidence, they tended to diagnose duodenal ulcer rather than dyspepsia. A false positive was arguably less risky (providing gastrectomy was avoided) than a false negative, given that perforation often led to death. Retrospective studies, based on mortality statistics, established that the war years witnessed an epidemic of peptic ulceration that subsequently rose to a peak prevalence in the-mid 1950s (Langman, 1979, p. 15). Such was the incidence of stomach disorders that two US military psychiatrists, Grinker and Spiegel, characterised World War Two as the gut war, which in their view contrasted with 'the frequent cardiac syndromes observed in the last war' (1945, pp. 108, 254–55).

However, recent research has suggested that the heart disorders of the late Nineteenth century had not disappeared by 1939 but had been reclassified. In 1917, Thomas Lewis proposed that DAH be re-named 'effort syndrome', because the symptoms could be replicated by 'a healthy person undertaking physical exercise' (Lewis, 1917, p. vi). Although some disagreed with this observation (Levine, 1965, p. 605), in the UK the term stuck. Not until 1941, following the seminal work of Paul Wood, a cardiologist based at Mill Hill EMS Hospital, was the true origin of effort syndrome identified (Wood, 1941a–c). Wood was assisted by advances in X-ray and ECG technology, together with an increasing understanding of research methodology. He was able to show that soldiers with a diagnosis of effort syndrome, when compared with controls, had a family history of significantly greater psychiatric morbidity. These findings encouraged military psychiatrists to attempt to treat cases of effort syndrome by re-education, occupational therapy and graduated exercise in contrast to the earlier emphasis on lengthy periods of bed rest and the avoidance of physical exertion. Although the new approach did not lead to any diminution of claims for war pensions characterized by medically unexplained symptoms, it did represent a different way of classifying post-combat disorders.

Furthermore, Wood explored the relationship between infection and the onset of so-called effort syndrome (1941c, p. 847). Of the 225 cases that he studied, 17 had been preceded by rheumatic fever, influenza, pneumonia and other fevers, while a further 29 had been aggravated by infection. However, Wood discovered that a greater number had been preceded by a traumatic event, including gassing, explosion, concussion or injury. 'The chief factor', he concluded (1941c, p. 847):

> 'was the belief, induced by the doctor, that the heart had been injured by the infection . . . It is therefore not surprising that rheumatic fever heads the list of these infections; influenza may come second because of the fallacious belief that it, too, injures the heart and because of its notorious influence on morale'.

By 1945, with data gathered from elite units (commandos, fighter squadrons and Royal Navy warships engaged on Artic convoys), it was recognized that every serviceman, however well trained and led, has his breaking point. It was also appreciated that stigma, considered by some a necessity in citizen armies to deter malingering, prevented soldiers from reporting psychiatric problems. As a result, military physicians needed to be alert to somatic symptoms that might have a psychological origin.

## Korean War

During the 1950s it appeared that the problem of the post-combat disorder had been solved by the growth in medical and psychiatric knowledge acquired during World War Two. Although large numbers of British troops were deployed to Korea (1951–53), no epidemic of war syndromes was reported. After an initial management blunder, when soldiers were flown to Kure, Japan, for treatment, men with unexplained medical symptoms were retained in theatre for investigation. Although both hospital and case notes have been destroyed, anecdotal evidence suggests there was no new variety of post-combat disorder and that claims for war pensions remained comparatively small.

## Vietnam

The Vietnam War (1961–1975), the longest conflict that American forces have fought, represented a turning point in the way that the psychological effects of war were perceived. It gave rise to a new diagnosis that, unlike shellshock, was also applied to civilians. Originally called 'post-Vietnam syndrome' or 'delayed stress disorder', it was admitted to the American Psychiatric Classification, *DSM-III*, as post-traumatic stress disorder (PTSD) in 1980 (American Psychiatric Association *DSM-III*, 1980, pp. 236–39). The emphasis, which had hitherto been placed on the individual's pre-morbid personality or preparedness, was now placed on the traumatic event itself. Sufferers were thereby absolved from any blame or responsibility for their symptoms and the stigma associated with this psychiatric diagnosis was noticeably diminished. Because British troops were not deployed to Vietnam, the impact of PTSD in the UK was somewhat delayed. In time, however, British troops serving in Northern Ireland were diagnosed as suffering from the disorder as were veterans of the Falklands conflict of 1982.

## Gulf War

The Gulf War of 1991, though short and successful, exercised a major impact on the expression and interpretation of post-combat disorders. Ironically, fewer British lives were lost as a result of enemy action as by friendly fire incidents and road traffic accidents. A so-called 'Desert Storm syndrome' was identified by US veterans towards the end of 1991, characterised by a range of medically unexplained symptoms. British veterans began to complain of similar symptom clusters in the following year and speculation about causation ran rife when the government rapidly dismissed allegations of a new disease. Press interest grew and veterans' pressure groups, both in the UK and US, successfully enlisted the support of senior politicians. Under such scrutiny, Gulf War syndrome became a high-profile issue with political and medical dimensions. Considerable sums of money have been spent on either side of the Atlantic in an attempt to resolve questions of causation and in turn treatment. Although something of a consensus has emerged among the medical community in the last five years, this has not translated to the veterans themselves, their supporters and the media. The saga of Gulf War syndrome is perhaps the most complex fought over issue of modern military medicine. With the sole exception of shellshock, never before has such a military disorder aroused such intense feeling, entrenched positions and polarized debate.

## SHELLSHOCK AND GULF WAR SYNDROME COMPARED

Whilst not suggesting that they are the same disorder masquerading under a different name, nevertheless, it is instructive to compare the history and development of shellshock with that of Gulf War syndrome (GWS). How they arose, the causal explanations offered by both doctors and veterans, together with the ways that society and governments responded provide important information for the management of future post-combat disorders.

### Origins

Crucially, both shellshock and GWS took the medical authorities by surprise. Few, if any, were prepared for either phenomenon and at first most struggled to understand their nature. Although the term 'shellshock' was first employed in a medical publication by Lt Colonel C.S. Myers, Consulting Psychologist to the BEF, in February 1915, he admitted that it was not of his making (Myers, 1915; 1940). Like GWS, it arose in common usage, rapidly caught popular imagination and has continued to have a lasting appeal (Leese, 2002). Typically soldiers diagnosed with shellshock complained of fatigue, poor sleep, nightmares, jumpiness, and had a variety of somatic symptoms such as palpitations, chest pain, tremor, joint and muscle pains, loss of voice or hearing and functional paralysis (Myers, 1916). Hence, both shellshock and GWS are characterised by a range of common medical symptoms, often leading to diverse but inconclusive inferences. Medical investigations have failed to discover any pathognomonic signs and in neither case has it been possible to devise a succinct and exclusive definition (Lee *et al.*, 2001, 2002).

### Explanations

Not surprisingly given the nature of the symptoms, explanations attached to shellshock and GWS are of a diverse nature. At first, shellshock was categorized by the military authorities as a physical wound. Frederick Mott, the eminent neuropathologist, proposed that it was a form of 'commotio cerebri' and hypothesised that the forces of compression and decompression, resulting from proximity to an explosion, in turn led to microscopic brain haemorrhage (Mott, 1916a,b). He also believed that carbon monoxide released by the blast might lead to cerebral poisoning. Mott was not alone in advancing a physical explanation and others suggested that the force of an explosion might have triggered epilepsy in previously healthy individuals or that it might be a consequence of venereal disease (Anon, 1916, p. 306).

Thomas Lewis, who primarily investigated cardiac abnormalities, observed clinical similarities between DAH and shellshock. He added a further list of possible organic causes including decreased buffer salts in the blood, an increased leucocyte count, and a difference in urinary constituents (increased calcium and oxalic acid together with decreased urea) (Lewis, 1917; Christophers, 1997). Early in 1916, Sir James Mackenzie argued that the privations of trench warfare not only weakened a man's constitution but also provided a suitable habitat for toxic bacteria (Mackenzie, 1916). The net result, he believed, was a state of general exhaustion and the heart abnormalities were not cardiac in origin, but the outcome of injury to the central nervous system (Wooley, 1986). Thus, like GWS, shellshock attracted a range of plausible medical explanations, which reflected the research interests of the investigator.

When it became apparent that many soldiers with the symptoms of shellshock had not been close to an explosion, and some not even in combat, a 'psychical' explanation was proposed (Elliot Smith, 1916, p. 817). Even Mott acknowledged the possibility of a second category to describe individuals with a vulnerability to stress and who could be so affected by the intense pressures of combat as to 'be rendered unconscious or so dazed as to necessitate them being taken or carried to the clearing station' (Mott, 1919, p. 439). Captain Harold Wiltshire, who until August 1915 had been responsible for the diagnosis of functional somatic cases at No. 12 General Hospital in Rouen, observed that (Wiltshire, 1916, p. 1212):

'In the vast majority of cases of shellshock, the exciting cause is some special psychic shock. Horrible sights are the most frequent and potent factor in the production of this shock. Losses and the fright of being buried are also important in this respect'.

The range of explanations proposed for GWS has, if anything, been broader than that for shellshock. These have included: fumes from burning oil wells, vaccinations, NAPS tablets (pyridostigmine bromide), the effects of organophosphate fertilizers, depleted uranium armaments, chemical or biological weapons, and the intense stress of combat. Although these were not the same explanations as had been proposed for shellshock, there are some historical parallels.

Suspicion of immunisation goes back to the Victorian period, when an anti-vaccination movement developed in Nineteenth-century Britain, driven in part by fear of intrusive government. As a response to the compulsory vaccination act of 1853, the movement rapidly became absorbed within alternative medicine, where practitioners argued that immunisation was a form of blood poisoning and that individuals could protect themselves against smallpox and other diseases by cleanliness, wholesome foods and fresh air (Durbach, 2005). As such it could be viewed as a reaction to professionalisation of orthodox medicine. Anti-vaccination campaigners were predominantly working and lower-middle class, finding allies in radical political groups.

In fact, the first modern vaccines applied on a mass scale were for typhoid in the British and French Armies during World War One (Moulin, 2000). British troops were routinely given anti-typhoid vaccination before being deployed to France. It has been suggested that tetanus was more widespread among British troops during World War One than in their French allies and German enemies because both Continental states had instituted an immunisation programme before the conflict. Pressure from the anti-vaccination movement had prevented such action in the UK. However, British medical authorities did authorise prophylactic use of tetanus antitoxin for wounded servicemen (Harrison, 2004). It was not until the late 1930s that the British Army routinely inoculated troops (Boyd, 1938). In the post-war period, the British exhibited a resistance to the *Bacillus Calmette-Guérin* vaccine (BCG) against tuberculosis, despite the fact it had been widely employed in France from the mid-1920s. Only when the Medical Research Council publicised its efficacy by a controlled trial in 1950 was prejudice overcome and an immunisation programme followed.

## Official Responses

Initially, the British military authorities gave shellshock the benefit of the doubt and sufferers were entitled to the award of a wound stripe. Soldiers discharged in 1916 with a diagnosis of shellshock were awarded war pensions, some at 100 %, though they may have been reduced subsequently. By March 1918, according to official records, 18 596 pensions (5.9 %) had been given for shellshock, neurasthenia and other nervous complaints. A further 33 343 (10.5 %) were awarded for cardiac disorders (largely the functional condition DAH), the third largest category after wounds to legs and chest complaints (Anon, 1919a, p. 140). In the 1920s, under pressure to cut expenditure, the Ministry of Pensions sought to curtail pensions for shellshock by regularly re-assessing veterans. Increasingly, the emphasis was on treatment for those with well-established symptoms. Because GWS has never been recognised as a legitimate medical diagnosis, it is not a pensionable disorder. However, by October 2001, 4111 war pensions had been awarded to veterans of the Gulf War, of which 1038 were for Gulf-related health issues.

In the latter part of 1919, the Ministry of Pensions set up a nationwide network of 'Special Medical Clinics' (to avoid the terms psychotherapeutic or cardiac). Where possible accommodation was sought 'in connection with an orthopaedic outpatient clinic' (Anon, 1919b). Difficulties were encountered not in finding suitable consulting rooms, but because of 'the scarcity of medical men who have received the training necessary for the treatment of these cases', and a training school was set up under Lt Colonel R.G. Rows, medical superintendent of Maghull (Anon, 1919c). By October 1920, 29 clinics were in operation. In February 1921, it was estimated that 14 771 ex-servicemen were either attending boards for assessment or clinics for treatment. As regards in-patients, the Ministry took over former military hospitals and, by October 1920, claimed to have 2809 beds for 'border-line shellshock and neurological cases' (Anon, 1920). By December 1925, the Ministry had re-structured its in-patient facilities to a national network of ten hospitals: Castle Leazes, Newcastle; Harrowby Camp, Grantham; Weard Camp, Saltash, Plymouth; Coombe Park, Bath; Ewell, Epsom; Orpington, Kent; Craigleith and Edenhall in Scotland; Craigavon, Northern Ireland, and Leopardstown Park, Dublin (Anon, 1925). According to official statistics, the number of patients treated by Ministry staff peaked in 1921 and declined steadily during the late 1920s and the 1930s. Although officials reported that hospital and clinic capacity consistently met the demand, the vast majority of veterans with psychological disorders were left to fend for themselves during the interwar period.

## Pressure Groups

Both shellshock and GWS caught the attention of veteran pressure groups. A number were set up towards the end of World War One largely driven by economic motives to improve the lot of the discharged serviceman. Key issues were delay in awarding war pensions and the amounts granted. Although none of the groups campaigned specifically on shellshock, the issue helped to enlist the support of MPs and the press. The idea that mentally scarred soldiers had not received adequate treatment or sufficient financial compensation to support their families stirred popular consciousness. In the event, the Ministry improved the administration of pensions and a significant rise in the level of awards was authorized in 1919.

In the spring of 1921, four ex-servicemen's pressure groups united to form the British Legion (Wootton, 1963). The amalgamation had been led by the National Federation of Discharged and Demobilised Sailors and Soldiers, aware that it had little future alone. At the annual conference in June, the leadership won a narrow victory in favour of union and invited the Comrades of the Great War, the National Association of Discharged Sailors and Soldiers, the National Union of Ex-Servicemen and the small but politically influential Officers' Association, to a meeting to consider merger (Latcham, 1997, p. 156). Only the National Union refused to consider the proposal in principle. At the Unity Conference held in May 1921, the British Legion was inaugurated (Wootton 1956, p. 26). One of its founding principles was to be 'democratic, non-sectarian and not affiliated to or connected directly or indirectly with any political party or political organisation', while another was to 'inculcate a sense of loyalty to the Crown, community and nation and to promote unity amongst all classes'. The formation of the Legion was not a feature of the strength of the veterans' movement but of its weakness. It began life with a membership of just 18 106 when 2 years earlier the Comrades and the Federation together accounted for something approaching 2 million members (Latcham, 1997, p. 160). It took a concerted drive to increase its numbers to over 100 000 by the following year. Only in 1938 did its membership exceed 400 000, and then it represented only 10 % of eligible veterans (Wootton, 1956, p. 305; Ward, 1975, p. 28).

Whilst veterans' pressure groups of WW1 campaigned on broad economic and social issues, their counterparts from the Gulf War had a more focused agenda. Believing that they were subject to a cover-up by the Ministry of Defence, and demanding effective treatment and compensation for their illnesses, groups of Gulf ex-servicemen held informal meetings. At a gathering held at Cramlington, Northumberland, in November 1994, the Gulf Veterans' Association (GVA) was formed. With the issue of Gulf War syndrome being then unresolved and claims for compensation outstanding, other organisations were formed, including the National Gulf Veterans' & Families' Association (NGVFA), based in Hull, which published a newsletter, *The Oasis Times*, and at one time claimed a national membership of 2000. VetNet was also linked to the NGVFA, as was the Gulf War Toxin Disease & Death Association. The Middle East Forces Veterans Association, a comrades' organisation set up by ex-servicemen from World War Two, took an interest in Gulf War veterans because both groups fought over the same battlefields. In addition, the Gulf War Veterans Trust, with links to the GVA, was registered as a private limited company and a charity. With their demands for improved medical treatment, compensation for damage to health and financial assistance with living costs, these UK veteran groups exhibit many of the characteristics of Vietnam-related US organisations of the 1970s.

As in the aftermath of World War One, the British Legion played a role in focusing and uniting disparate veteran groups. In April 1998, the GVA, VetNet and the Middle East Forces Veterans Association agreed to form a Gulf Veterans Royal British Legion Branch (GVB RBL) with a national network. Based in Newcastle-upon-Tyne, the GVB RBL shares premises with the GVA, and has sub-branches in Wales and Northern Ireland. Flight Lieutenant John Nichol, the ex-RAF navigator who was captured and tortured by Saddam Hussein's forces in the Gulf War, was elected president of the GVB. The NGVFA refused to join the GVB, remaining at odds with the Ministry of Defence over the health effects of depleted uranium in the Gulf. Although the British Legion may have moderated the more extreme demands of some veterans, its measured and evidence-based approach could be threatened in the future. Many of the Legion's members are veterans of World War Two, the Korean conflict and the era of National Service, and continue to express the cultural values of those times. Over the next few decades, the character of the British Legion's membership will change as smaller numbers of younger ex-servicemen, whose military experience relates to Northern Ireland, the Falklands, the Gulf, Ruanda, Bosnia and Kosovo, slowly form the majority. They, like their Vietnam counterparts, may prove to be more vociferous and less willing to compromise than were their predecessors.

## Summary

Shellshock became a recognised term during 1915, while Gulf War syndrome became established and spread in 1992–93, some 77 years later. To date, no new post-combat disorder has been attached to servicemen who served in Bosnia, Kosovo, Afghanistan or the Iraq War. Hence, a considerable time may pass before the appearance of the next war syndrome to take the medical and military authorities by surprise. There is no knowing what form it will take or how it will be described. We can, however, be certain that if it is to attract widespread attention, the disorder will have to strike a chord in popular consciousness and feed on widely shared health fears and beliefs. Military institutions do learn lessons, as the concerted campaign to avoid use of the term 'shell-shock' in 1939 demonstrated. However, as key individuals retire and new doctrines are introduced, experience and understanding can be lost. In such situations clusters of common symptoms can be misinterpreted as either a new or a unique disorder, although the advance of diag-nostic techniques continues to narrow the somatic field in which they can mislead. The introduction of endoscopy, for example, has effectively prevented the recurrence of mass discharges for suspected duodenal ulcer, and by permitting the accurate diagnosis of cardiac abnormalities the ECG has ruled out DAH and effort syndrome.

# CHANGING NATURE OF WARFARE

Two factors have exercised a major influence on the expression of post-combat disorders and the explanations given for their existence: (i) changing health beliefs, which are crucially tied to advances in medical science, and (ii) the changing technology of warfare together with devel-opments in tactics that new weapons systems allow.

## Boer War

Troops who fought in the Boer War were often required to march considerable distances to engage the enemy; it was a war of movement without mechanization. Contemporaries believed that the sustained physical exertion in a hot climate was, in part, responsible for the various heart disorders encountered. Indeed, an official report explained the high incidence of DAH in the orderlies of the newly formed Royal Army Medical Corps in terms of the great distances that field ambulance units were required to march to support infantry and cavalry (Wilson, 1904, p. 71). In the latter stages of the war, a large number of columns were deployed against Boer guerrilla units, so that medical units had long periods of continuous marching to keep up with the widely spread engagements. It was concluded that the prolonged strain of carrying heavy weights and the pressure of straps on the chest damaged the heart. The report also argued that 'cardiac exhaustion cases were much more frequent among men of volunteer companies than the regulars, probably due to the great difference of their usual daily occupation from the life of a soldier on active service' (Wilson, 1904, p. 73). Once a soldier had succumbed to DAH, it was noticed that the symptoms returned if he had to 'undergo any extra exertion, or from the excitement or nervousness of going under fire'. These cases also increased 'if the physical strength of the men cannot be kept up by good and sufficient food and the necessary amount of sleep and rest'. Thus, the important connection between what would be called acute stress reaction and continuous exposure to combat had been observed but its implications not fully understood.

According to official statistics, 2613 servicemen were admitted to military hospitals with VDH and a further 3631 with DAH during the Boer War; 73 % of the former and 41 % of the latter were invalided to the UK, where they were generally discharged (Mitchell and Smith, 1931, p. 273). In addition, 24 460 troops were hospitalised with rheumatic fever or rheumatism. The distinction between the two was not always accurately drawn. In addition, physicians believed that an adult who caught rheumatic fever would suffer permanent damage to the mitral or aortic valves and would therefore be likely to die prematurely from heart failure. In fact, rheumatic fever rarely causes long-term heart problems in individuals over the age of 16. A further factor that increased caution when dealing with soldiers exhibiting any cardiac abnormality was the absence of any form of treatment. In terms of surgery the heart was a no-go area. Even as late as 1943, Thomas Lewis argued that any attempt to address mitral stenosis surgically was both reckless and theoretically flawed. It was not until 1948 that Russell Brock at Guy's Hospital devised a procedure to correct constricted heart valves. Given that murmurs and palpitations could be indicative of a life-threatening disease and that there were no remedies, it is scarcely surprising that soldier's heart, DAH and, later, effort syndrome flourished among members of the armed forces.

A common and strongly held belief, expressed by both men and RAMC doctors during the Boer War, was that exposure to cold and wet on the veldt was the primary cause of rheumatic pains. A further 20 767 servicemen were hospitalised with debility, a chronic fatigue syndrome with no demonstrable organic cause, and 26 % were subsequently invalided to the UK. An analysis of war pensions administered by the Royal Hospital, Chelsea, which were largely awarded to veterans of the Boer War (Table 2.1), showed that though most were for gunshot wounds a significant percentage were for post-combat disorders characterised by functional somatic symptoms.

A random sample of 200 cases of DAH/VDH and 200 cases of rheumatism from all surviving Boer War pension files, revealed that 40.5 % and 38.5 % respectively had been admitted for a recognized illness (largely enteric fever or dysentery) before developing a post-combat disorder. To what extent earlier symptoms were elaborated or replaced is not known because of the loss or destruction of in-patient medical records. However, as Hyams *et al.* (1996) observed, contemporary accounts established a link between war syndromes characterized by unexplained symptoms and infectious disease. If, as Kilshaw (2004) has suggested, post-combat disorders represent a narrative or coded

Table 2.1    An analysis of pensions awarded by the Royal Hospital, Chelsea (1854–1913)

| Disorder | As a single diagnosis | As part of a multiple diagnosis |
|---|---|---|
| Disordered Action of the Heart (DAH) | 132 (2.1 %) | 199 (3.2 %) |
| Valvular Disease of the Heart (VDH) | 244 (3.9 %) | 356 (5.7 %) |
| Rheumatism | 158 (2.5 %) | 272 (4.3 %) |
| Debility | 89 (1.4 %) | 392 (6.2 %) |
| Schizophrenia and delusional state | 9 (0.1 %) | 9 (0.1 %) |
| Manic-depressive psychosis | 16 (0.3 %) | 18 (0.3 %) |
| Depression | 22 (0.4 %) | 23 (0.4 %) |
| Neurasthenia/ nervous weakness | 11 (0.2 %) | 20 (0.3 %) |
| Gunshot wounds | 2218 (35.3 %) | 2268 (36.1 %) |
| Other diagnoses | 3021 (48.1 %) | NA |
| Not recorded | 356 (5.7 %) | 356 (5.7 %) |
| Total | 6276 (100 %) | 6276 (100 %) |

Source: PRO, PIN71/1-6276: War Pension Files from the Royal Hospital, Chelsea. Reproduced with permission of the British Journal of Psychiatry.

form of communication, it is possible that some of the vocabulary was learnt while a patient in a military hospital.

## World War One

Shellshock was framed in terms of trench warfare: an expression of the terror felt by men forced to endure passively the effects of artillery bombardment (Shephard, 2000). From an early stage in the war, industrial capabilities produced a stalemate in military tactics as troops on both sides dug increasingly elaborate positions to protect themselves against attack. The machine gun, when placed behind barbed wire and supported by artillery, provided a formidable defensive capability. The only effective offensive weapon available to armies throughout the entire conflict was the artillery barrage. Although concentrated shelling could open a gap in a fortified line, transport limitations prevented heavy artillery from being moved in support of advancing infantry, and attacks tended to peter out once they had gained a few miles. Without reliable communications technology (telephone lines were easily disrupted), commanders had rudimentary, and often delayed, contact with their forces. For the most part, World War One was a conflict of attrition with limited 'bite and hold' attacks designed to wear down the enemy. Only in the latter stages were attempts made to coordinate artillery, tanks and infantry, partly by use of spotter aircraft, and to raise the technical skills of infantry platoons to include Lewis gunners and mortar teams.

Because of difficulties in moving heavy guns quickly, the British army could only achieve concentrated artillery fire by greatly increasing the number of batteries and the supply of shells to them. In 1918, for example, the diversion of industrial production to munitions resulted in the manufacture of 10 680 new guns, compared with 3226 in 1915. At the end of the war the Royal Artillery mustered half a million men and represented a quarter of the British Army (Strachan, 2003, p. 307). The 'combined-arms battle', which brought victory in November 1918, was built around the capabilities of the artillery rather than the infantry. A short intense barrage was designed to disorientate the enemy, damage his defensive positions and on occasion to catch him by surprise. The creeping barrage that followed gave the advancing infantry cover and protected them from counter-attack. First, second and third lines of defence could be isolated from each other by curtains of fire. Cut off from re-supply or reinforcements, the isolation felt by defenders added to the terrors of bombardment itself.

Hand-to-hand fighting was rare during the First World War and most killing was impersonal. Fifty-nine per cent of wounds inflicted on British soldiers were as a result of artillery, and three times as many men were killed by shells as by bullets (Sheffield, 2001). Given the significance of artillery and its dominance of the battlefield, whether in static trenches or mobile offensives, it scarcely surprising that the dominant post-combat disorder of World War One was shellshock. Furthermore, casualty rates amongst front-line units were so high during offensives that primary groups were quickly destroyed. The British army suffered 705 000 fatalities and 1.2 million wounded. Compared with these statistics, losses in World War Two (144 000 killed and 425 500 wounded, missing or taken prisoner) were significant but much lower (French, 2000). Casualties amongst British troops deployed to the Gulf were of a different order of magnitude: 47 fatalities of which many were road traffic accidents and 9 as the result of so-called 'friendly fire'.

Whilst wounds and preventing the spread of infection, largely gangrene, preoccupied military medicine during World War One, the arrival of an apparently devastating novel weapon, gas, produced a new set of clinical imperatives. Not only did the introduction of chemical weapons lead to a significant diversion of medical resources, it also led to a new diagnosis: 'gas hysteria'.

By 1916, doctors had become acutely aware of the power of gas to create invalidity in men who had only mild exposures. Following the first chlorine attacks, great emphasis was placed on rest and unexplained cardiac symptoms were attributed to excessive physical exercise (Sloggett, 1916, p. 14). Severe cases were to be retained at casualty clearing stations for at least 4 days and transferred to base hospitals lying down. A study by Lt Colonel S.L. Cummins and Major T.R. Elliott, based on 600 cases in convalescent depots in France during May and June 1916, concluded that 'there is a state of cardiac disability, similar to "soldier's irritable heart", which may be caused by drift gas poisoning; and it is most likely that undue haste in physical training during convalescence may aggravate the condition' (Cummins and Elliott, 1916, p. 6). A report compiled in autumn 1916 showed that even moderate cases were commonly in medical units for 2 to 3 months 'and very possibly longer' (Elliott and Douglas, 1916, p. 13). As a result, fertile conditions were created for the elaboration of symptoms and chronic invalidity.

Although, the introduction of oxygen therapy saved lives and reduced recovery times of those who had been gassed (Haldane, 1917), it had no lasting or therapeutic effect on chronic cases reclassified as DAH (Haldane *et al.*, 1918, p.1; Barcroft *et al.*, 1918, pp. 16–17). Without an obvious treatment, the belief pervaded the British medical service in France that 'gas poisoning causes such prolonged invalidism that the casualties had better be evacuated at once to the UK' (Elliott, 1918). Indeed, an analysis of all gas cases admitted between 1st July and 31st October 1917 showed that 58 % were evacuated to the UK and only 23 % returned to some form of duty in France (Douglas, 1918a, p. 1). Concerned by lengthy stays in medical units and the need to return as many soldiers as possible to fighting units, Douglas, Elliott and Soltau studied gassed patients at various stages in their treatment (from field ambulance to casualty clearing station, base hospitals and convalescent depots in France, and cases evacuated to the UK) to record lengths of admission and outcomes. Key points in treatment were identified when so-called 'neurasthenic' symptoms might develop (Douglas, 1918a, p. 33). Strategies were developed to maintain the momentum of recovery and to distract patients from their symptoms. For example, men wearing dark glasses to combat the effects of photophobia were ordered to remove them once their pupils had returned to a normal size and colour (Lister, 1918).

Because few doctors had any training in the treatment of chemical weapons, and few could reliably distinguish types of gas from presenting symptoms, specialist gas units were established. As late as April 1918, Lt Colonel C.G. Douglas, a physiologist attached to the British Expeditionary Force, observed: 'I really believe that nearly all medical officers are terrified by the mere mention of gas poisoning' (Douglas, 1918b). This led to defensive medicine by which cases were referred to base hospitals, often in the UK (Douglas, 1918c). This transit of men to the rear not only reduced the number likely to return to active duty, but it also reinforced the idea in patients' minds that the effects of gas were serious and long lasting Lister, 1918.

## World War Two

During World War One, regular officers had doubted that volunteers and later conscripts could be trained in little more than rudimentary military skills. At the outset, therefore, they were taught only drill to instill discipline, and target practice. However, from 1917 onwards, when the distinction between professional soldiers and other troops had effectively disappeared, units were trained in more sophisticated attacking methods, involving a range of coordinated weapons. In the semi-mobile war from August 1918, the so-called 'Hundred Days', many of the offensive techniques that were routinely practiced by infantry during World War Two had been worked out (Sheffield, 2001, pp. 245–46, 259). By 1939, technological advances were in place that gave tanks and armoured cars greater reliability and range. Moreover, infantry and artillery were increasingly mechanized to allow them to keep pace with the armour. With these developments, the German army was able to develop the *Blitzkrieg*, a tactic later adopted by the Soviets on the Eastern Front. Apart from the design of more powerful and reliable engines to drive tanks and haul guns, a significant technological advance occurred in radio communications. High-powered radios enabled a measure of voice control to return to the battlefield. Once again commanders had the ability to exploit opportunities and vigorously pursue a retreating enemy.

It would be wrong, however, to characterize World War Two solely as a conflict of movement. A number of important battles were static, such as Stalingrad, Cassino and Normandy. Whatever the form of the engagement, artillery continued to dominate in all theatres. Despite popular impressions, casualty rates were sometimes far higher than in World War One. The average loss rate for British and Canadian infantry battalions on the Western Front was about 100 per month. In the campaign in northwest Europe, from D-Day to the end of the war in May 1945, battalions suffered a minimum of 100 casualties a month, and rates of 175 were not uncommon (Sheffield, 2001, p. 276). Despite popular belief, routine trench warfare was not associated with high casualties. Large numbers of killed and wounded arose in both World Wars when troops attacked well-defended positions. Of the 55 officers of the 1st Battalion of the Gordon Highlanders who commanded rifle platoons in operations following the Normandy invasion, 53 % were wounded, 24 % invalided and only 5 % survived their tour of duty in north-west Europe (Lindsay, 2000).

In the air, technological advance was particularly apparent. Faster, more aerobatic, fighters and larger more reliable bombers, both with increased range, changed the character of the war. Civilians were drawn into the front-line and artillery barrages could be supported by intense bombing raids, as at Cassino. Air combat produced its own varieties of post-combat disorder: 'flying stress', 'aviation neurasthenia' had been coined during World War One and were initially attributed to anoxia, the result of flying in rarified air. In March 1940, the Royal Air Force introduced a new term 'lack of moral fibre' (LMF), which was designed to deter aircrew from refusing to fly without a sound medical reason (Jones, 2006). Aircrew given the label 'LMF' were deliberately stigmatised; they lost their flying badges and were sent to a network of 'Not Yet Diagnosed, Neuropsychiatric' Centres for assessment and treatment. Those who failed to return to operational duty were discharged from the air force, reduced to the ranks, or transferred to the army. Although the final decision was taken by the Air Council, the system crucially relied on information supplied by the squadron medical officer and the psychiatric assessor at an NYDN Centre.

Although the label was formally restricted to the RAF, it was used informally for a brief period by the army in the Western Desert (Harrison, 2004). However, it was not popular with servicemen or doctors and fell out of use. Indeed, the procedure introduced in March 1940 was subject to a sustained campaign of criticism by RAF doctors. Air Commodore Charles Symonds (1890–1978) and Group Captain Robert Gillespie (1897–1945), a neurologist and psychiatrist respectively, who had been recruited on the outbreak of war, argued that the stigmatising process, designed to serve as a deterrent, failed to distinguish between the pilot who gave up on his first training flight and the decorated veteran exhausted by the stress of a second tour. As a result, detailed studies were undertaken by Symonds, assisted by Denis Williams, of the various Commands to investigate the relationship between flying stress and particular roles, types of aircraft and tours of duty (Symonds, 1943a, b). Although modifications were made to the 'LMF' system, it remained in existence until the end of the war. The highest breakdown rates were recorded in Bomber Command where crews suffered the highest casualties in situations where they could do little to defend themselves. It was a policy driven, as David Stafford-Clark, himself a former squadron medical officer, stated, by the belief that 'true combat volunteers could not be "cowards" ', and as a result the penalties within the system were often 'very harsh indeed' (Stafford Clark, p. 43); whether they were truly necessary remains a moot question.

## Post-1945

The pace of technological change in the military has quickened dramatically following the arrival of the helicopter, the jet engine (to power both missiles and aircraft), and the application of computers to both weapon and communication systems. Mechanisation and Chobham armour have allowed troops and artillery to be deployed more rapidly and in greater safety than ever before. The development of increasingly accurate and intense firepower has broadened the capability gap between NATO nations and other armed forces. This, in turn, has shortened the length of major conflicts. By comparison, peacekeeping operations, which have proliferated, tend to be much longer-term commitments.

Changes in the nature of conflict and the increasing use of air transport have cut preparation times and reduced opportunities for troops to wind down from hazardous operations. For example, a soldier might be on exercise in Salisbury Plain and a week later find himself serving in the deserts of the Middle East. Troops are routinely flown from RAF Brize Norton to Afghanistan, Iraq, the Falklands and the Balkans. The return to the UK can also be equally swift. Even veterans of World War Two, who travelled home at sedate pace in troopships, found the transition from active service to civilian life difficult to manage. Some servicemen took the option of an overseas posting (designed to stagger the mass demobilization of conscripts) once the peace had been signed, or joined the Territorial Army as a way of adjusting to a radically different lifestyle.

The certainty that went with Cold War planning has passed and today, according to General Walker, Chief of the Defence Staff (Walker, 2005, pp. 45–46):

'We often do not even know who the enemy is, much less where. When he does emerge it is often in inhospitable and remote parts of the world. We see him fleetingly. He emerges briefly, strikes and disappears ... It is hard to envisage anything more starkly different from the symmetrical, land, air and maritime battle of attrition that we used to plan for in the Cold War'.

As a result the British Army is in a state of transition: from a continental force designed to delay and wear down a mass tank invasion, into an expeditionary-based army optimized for rapid intervention overseas.

Although professional soldiers are better protected than ever before with flak jackets, NBC suits, vaccination programmes and armoured vehicles, they are also at risk from a greater range of more potent weapons. Whilst the pace of warfare has quickened and its technical complexity advanced, at root, combat still involves soldiers risking their lives. In its fundamentals, the stress of battle has not changed, as troops in the teeth of arms are still required to kill or be killed.

## Exposure to Combat

To test whether the form of post-combat disorders has changed over time, Jones *et al.* (2002) selected random samples of war pensioners from all major wars from 1900 to the Gulf. Although the primary aim of the study was to explore symptom clusters (see below), it also investigated each subject's experience of combat. An analysis of the military records of servicemen in our study, together with war diaries, revealed that the proportion involved in actual fighting fell over time as the proportion of troops in combat-support roles has risen. Of the Boer War veterans, 77 % had been in combat, of the World War One pensioners 73.4 %, of the World War Two sample 52 %, while only 19.8 % of the Gulf War sample had seen action. War syndromes arose, therefore, not only in servicemen who fought but also in those faced with the prospect of battle.

Furthermore, post-combat disorders were not just suffered by teeth arms, which comprised the infantry, artillery, cavalry/armour, engineers and signals. They were also reported in combat-support troops, soldiers who provided vital services to those in the front line: drivers, cooks, paymasters, intelligence, education, and supplies. Furthermore, non-combatant units, which were not expected to fight, though were some-times exposed to combat and included medical services and unarmed pioneer or labour companies, suffered their effects.

It has been hypothesised that troops in supportive roles, often isolated or denied the protection of a close-knit group, were more prone to stress reactions, though typically exposed to less intense fighting (Glass, 1973). Taking the samples in the study by Jones *et al.* (2002), these were analysed by type of unit, whether combatant, combat support and non-combatant (Table 2.2). At first sight, the results do not confirm Glass' hypothesis, as 92.3 % of the Boer War samples, 84.3 % of the World War One groups and 70.3 % of the World War Two samples were from combat units. However, these statistics reflected the changing shape of the armed forces. In August 1914, 92.8 % of Britain's 500 000 regular army was composed of combat troops, while combat support units accounted for only 3.5 % (Anon, *Statistics of the Military Effort*, 1922, p. 28). By November 1918, when the strength of the British army had risen to 3 759 470, the proportions had changed significantly in response

Table 2.2   Units

| War – disorder | All units | | |
|---|---|---|---|
| | Combat | Combat support | Non-combat |
| *Victorian campaigns* | | | |
| (1) Cardiac | 18 (94.7) | 0 | 1 (5.3) |
| (2) Debility | 7 (77.8) | 1 (11.1) | 1 (11.1) |
| *Boer War* | | | |
| (1) DAH | 184 (92) | 8 (4) | 8 (4) |
| (2) Rheumatism | 185 (92.5) | 5 (2.5) | 10 (5) |
| *World War One* | | | |
| (1) DAH | 173 (86.5) | 20 (10) | 7 (3.5) |
| (2) Neurasthenia | 164 (82) | 28 (14) | 8 (4) |
| (3) Gassed | 152 (91) | 9 (5.4) | 6 (3.6) |
| (4) Nurses | 0 | 0 | 73 (100) |
| *World War Two* | | | |
| (1) Effort syndrome | 41 (61.2) | 22 (32.8) | 4 (6) |
| (2) Psychoneurosis | 154 (77) | 40 (20) | 6 (3) |
| (3) Dyspepsia | 72 (72) | 24 (24) | 4 (4) |
| *Korea/Malaya* | | | |
| (1) Psychoneurosis | 10 (66.7) | 4 (26.7) | 1 (6.6) |
| (2) Dyspepsia | 2 (40) | 3 (60) | 0 |
| (3) Effort syndrome | 1 (100) | 0 | 0 |
| *Gulf War* | | | |
| Gulf-related illness | 215 (53.8) | 130 (32.5) | 55 (13.7) |
| TOTAL | 1, 378   (73.9) | 294   (15.8) | 184 (9.9) |

to the increasingly technical nature of war and the need for a long logistics tail to supply mass armies: combat troops accounted for 74.9 %, combat support 20.5 % and non-combatant were 4.5 % (*Statistics of the Military Effort*, 1922, p. 231). The proportion of teeth arms in the Middle East Force, which fought in the Western Desert between 1942 and 1943, had fallen to 63 % (James, 1955, p. 106). For the Boer War and World War One, the percentages are not greatly at variance with the overall composition of the armed forces. Historically, combat-support units grew absolutely and proportionately as war became more technical, while medical services developed in tune with scientific advance. The Gulf War sample showed a distinct difference from the earlier pattern as only 53.8 % were from combat units and 32.5 % from combat support. In practice, however, many regular combat troops in the Gulf were required to undertake support roles because of the greatly reduced size of the British army. The changing composition of the armed forces can explain only part of this phenomenon.

## Attributions by Servicemen

How, then, did servicemen themselves explain their war syndromes? Applicants for a war pension were required to state what they thought was the cause of their disability (Jones and Wessely, 2005). In addition, doctors recorded patient statements at subsequent assessments. In the main, there were six categories of explanation: (i) that symptoms were the result of a physical illness acquired while in the army; (ii) the result either of a physical injury or the physical strain of campaigning (marching, sleeping on hard ground, completing assault courses); (iii) the result of an adverse climate (wet and cold in South Africa) or environment (the heat of the Western Desert or monsoon jungle of Burma); (iv) the result of a toxic exposure: either to gas in First World War or chemical and biological weapons or depleted uranium ordnance in the Gulf War; (v) the result of psychological stress caused by combat or the prospect of combat; (vi) the result of psychological stress caused by distance from family and friends or particular home worries.

An analysis of pensioners' explanations suggested that attributions were culturally conditioned and varied across the century, tied to prevailing health beliefs and concerns (Table 2.3). Boer War servicemen diagnosed with DAH generally believed it to be the result of either physical illness (25.5 %) or of physical exertion (24.5 %). A different pattern emerged in World War One with physical exertion accounting for 45.0 % of the DAH sample and 42.5 % of the neurasthenia group. However, a significant number of the latter (34.0 %) attributed their symptoms to the psychological stress of military service. They had, perhaps, been influenced by psychologically minded physicians, and the gradual incursion of psychiatric texts into medical and general literature.

World War Two saw this process continue and 41.0 % of the neuropsychiatric sample attributed their symptoms to psychological stress arising from military service, and a further 5 % to stresses related to their domestic situation. By contrast, 44.0 % of the dyspepsia population ascribed their symptoms to the physical exertions of active service, as did 52.5 % of the effort syndrome sample. Only 8.3 % of the Gulf War sample believed that stress played a causal role, while 61.3 % thought that their condition was connected with some form of toxic exposure.

Contemporary attributions made by servicemen broadly correlated with the symptom characteristics (Young, 1995) of the three groups. In the debility cluster, 61.2 % believed that their illness was related to a physical illness, to physical injury/strain, climate or toxic exposure. By comparison, 143 (63.8 %) of the 224 who believed the psychological

Table 2.3  Attributions by servicemen

| War/Disorder | Physical illness | Injury or physical strain | Climate – environment | Toxic exposure | Psychological stress service | Psychological stress domestic | Not reported | Total |
|---|---|---|---|---|---|---|---|---|
| *Victorian campaigns* | | | | | | | | |
| 1. Cardiac | 5 (26.3) | 4 (21.1) | 2 (10.5) | 0 | 0 | 0 | 8 (42.1) | 19 (100) |
| 2. Debility | 0 | 2 (22.2) | 3 (33.3) | 0 | 0 | 0 | 4 (44.5) | 9 (100) |
| *Boer War* | | | | | | | | |
| 1. DAH | 51 (25.5) | 49 (24.5) | 22 (11) | 0 | 2 (1) | 0 | 76 (38) | 200 (100) |
| 2. Rheum | 35 (17.5) | 30 (15) | 74 (37) | 0 | 2 (1) | 0 | 59 (29.5) | 200 (100) |
| *World War 1* | | | | | | | | |
| 1. DAH | 35 (17.5) | 90 (45) | 12 (6) | 3 (1.5) | 8 (4) | 0 | 52 (26) | 200 (100) |
| 2. Neur | 11 (5.5) | 85 (42.5) | 4 (2) | 3 (1.5) | 68 (34) | 1 (0.5) | 28 (14) | 200 (100) |
| 3. Gassed | 1 (0.5) | 12 (7.2) | 0 | 141 (84.95) | 2 (1.2) | 0 | 11 (6.6) | 163 (100) |
| *Nurses* | | | | | | | | |
| 1. DAH | 9 (37.5) | 8 (33.3) | 2 (8.3) | 0 | 0 | 0 | 5 (20.9) | 24 (100) |
| 2. Neur | 10 (20.4) | 20 (40.8) | 3 (6.1) | 0 | 6 (12.2) | 2 (4.0) | 8 (16.5) | 49 (100) |
| *World War 2* | | | | | | | | |
| 1. Effort | 5 (7.5) | 25 (37.3) | 5 (7.5) | 1 (1.5) | 14 (20.9) | 6 (9) | 11 (16.3) | 67 (100) |
| 2. Psych. | 9 (4.5) | 65 (32.5) | 7 (3.5) | 1 (0.5) | 82 (41) | 10 (5) | 26 (13) | 200 (100) |
| 3. Dyspepsia | 12 (12) | 44 (44) | 10 (10) | 0 | 5 (5) | 0 | 29 (29) | 100 (100) |

Table 2.3 (Continued)

| War/ Disorder | Physical illness | Injury or physical strain | Climate – environment | Toxic exposure | Psychological stress service | Psychological stress domestic | Not reported | Total |
|---|---|---|---|---|---|---|---|---|
| *Korea/ Malaya* | | | | | | | | |
| 1. Psych | 2 (13.3) | 3 (15) | 1 (6.7) | 0 | 2 (13.3) | 5 (33.4) | 2 (13.3) | 15 (100) |
| 2. Dyspepsia | 0 | 3 (60) | 0 | 0 | 0 | 1 (20) | 1 (20) | 5 (100) |
| 3. Effort | 0 | 1 (100) | 0 | 0 | 0 | 0 | 0 | 1 (100) |
| *Gulf War* | | | | | | | | |
| Gulf related illness | 1 (0.3) | 9 (2.2) | 0 | 245 (61.3) | 33 (8.3) | 2 (0.5) | 110 (27.5) | 400 (100) |
| TOTAL | 186 | 450 | 145 | 394 | 224 | 27 | 430 | 1856 |

Reproduced with permission from Jones and Wessely (2005), War syndromes: the impact of culture on medically unexplained symptoms, *Medical History*, 49, 75.

stress of military service was the cause of their illness came from the neuropsychiatric cluster. Equally, only 23 (12.4 %) of the 186 who believed that they were suffering from a physical illness were found in this group.

## Veterans and Employment

What, then, happened to servicemen with post-combat syndromes once they had been discharged from the army and had been awarded a war pension? The files of 1865 subjects were examined to discover how many were able to return to paid employment, and how many were so disabled by their symptoms that they were not offered jobs or felt obliged to resign once in post (Jones *et al.*, 2001). Some 77 % of Boer War veterans in the two samples returned to paid employment, while 22 % were either unable or unwilling to work (Table 2.4). The proportion

**Table 2.4** Veterans and employment

| War – Disorder | Working | Not working | Not known |
| --- | --- | --- | --- |
| *Victorian campaigns* | | | |
| (1) Cardiac | 6 (66.6) | 0 | 3 (33.4) |
| (2) Debility | 18 (94.7) | 0 | 1 (5.3) |
| *Boer War* | | | |
| (1) DAH | 154 (77) | 43 (21.5) | 3 (1.5) |
| (2) Rheumatism | 153 (76.5) | 46 (23) | 1 (0.5) |
| *World War One* | | | |
| (1) DAH | 89 (44.5) | 8 (4) | 103 (51.5) |
| (2) Neurasthenia | 95 (47.5) | 7 (3.5) | 98 (49) |
| (3) Gassed | 49 (29.3) | 30 (18.0) | 88 (52.7) |
| Nurses | | | |
| (4) DAH | 7 (29.2) | 9 (37.5) | 8 (66.7) |
| (5) Neurasthenia | 16 (32.7) | 20 (40.8) | 13 (26.5) |
| *World War Two* | | | |
| (1) Effort syndrome | 56 (83.6) | 3 (4.5) | 8 (11.9) |
| (2) Psychoneurosis | 154 (77) | 11 (5.5) | 13 (13) |
| (3) Dyspepsia | 85(85) | 2(2) | 13(13) |
| *Korea/Malaya* | | | |
| (1) Psychoneurosis | 9 (60) | 1 (6.7) | 5 (33.3) |
| (2) Dyspepsia | 5 (100) | 0 | 0 |
| (3) Effort syndrome | 1 (100) | 0 | 0 |
| *Gulf War* | | | |
| Gulf-related illness | 253 (63.3) | 30 (7.5) | 117 (29.3) |
| TOTAL | 1150 (61.7) | 210 (11.3) | 496 (26.6) |

known to have gone back to employment after World War One was noticeably lower (46 %). This was, in part, a function of nature of war pension files, which did not systematically record a veteran's work status. Despite the harsh economic climate of the 1920s and the deep post-war depression, only 4 % were known not to be able to work. Under pressure from MPs and veterans' pressure groups, the Ministry of Pensions introduced re-training schemes for ex-servicemen, who were also given priority by some employers. The vast majority of veterans from the World War Two samples (80%) returned to jobs after 1945. Similarly, most of the Gulf population (63%) were either employed in civilian life or continued to serve in the army. Only 8% were definitely unable to work.

## CONCLUSIONS

When assessed by their characteristic symptoms, no single post-combat disorder could be identified as being common to all modern wars (Jones *et al.*, 2001). It appears that different varieties arise in response to changing circumstances. The form that these take is chiefly determined by the chronology of the associated war framed either by a gap in medical knowledge (soldier's heart, DAH, effort syndrome and non-ulcer dyspepsia) or by a particular characteristic of warfare (shellshock or Agent Orange syndrome). Whilst gaps in medical knowledge are constantly being closed, technical evolution proceeds at a pace. It is possible, therefore, that any future post-combat disorder will assume a form or explanation based in novel or disputed science.

Rapid deployment and the uncertainties of modern warfare suggest that future medical emphasis will be on well-established psychiatric diagnoses such as PTSD, substance abuse, and depression, rather than post-combat disorders characterised by somatic symptoms. Whilst treatments are in place to deal with psychiatric diagnoses (CBT and SSRI anti-depressants for PTSD), it is less certain how to address war syndromes. Once established, symptoms appear to be resistant to change. A wide variety of approaches has been attempted in the past, including bed rest followed by graduated exercise, re-education and group therapy, electric shock treatment, occupational therapy, individual therapy, abreaction, hypnotism and insulin-coma therapy. None of these methods was evaluated by a random-controlled trial and we remain reliant on case reports or outcome studies that rarely include follow-ups. Although no method appears to offer an effective solution in terms of symptom relief, of the

1360 subjects in our study about whom we had employment data, 85 % returned to some form of work after military service.

Because post-combat syndromes have arisen after all major wars over the last century, we can predict that new examples will appear at some time in the future, though we cannot forecast what form they will assume. Because war syndromes have been recognised as pensionable disorders and proved difficult to treat, they have cost governments considerable sums in financial assistance. In order to introduce preventative measures and devise effective clinical interventions, it is necessary to understand their characteristics. If each new post-combat syndrome is not interpreted as a unique or novel illness, but as part of an understandable pattern of normal responses to the physical and psychological stress of war, then it may plausibly be managed in a more effective manner.

# REFERENCES

Anon (1912). *Report of the Army Medical Department*, London: HMSO.

Anon (1916). A discussion of shellshock, *Lancet*, i, 306.

Anon (1919a) *First Annual Report of the Minister of Pensions to 31 March 1918*. London: HMSO.

Anon (1919b). Letter from A. Webb, Director General of Medical Services, Ministry of Pensions, (Public Record Office (hereafter PRO), PIN15/55, Treatment of Neurasthenia).

Anon (1919c). Letter from Director General of Medical Services, Ministry of Pensions, (PRO, PIN15/55, Treatment of Neurasthenia, 18 December 1919).

Anon (1920). Accommodation for border-line cases, *Lancet*, ii, 923.

Anon (1922). *Statistics of the Military Effort of the British Empire during the Great War*, London: HMSO.

Anon (1925). Answer to parliamentary question, 15 December 1925 (PRO, PIN15/2946/81).

American Psychiatric Association (1980), *Diagnostic and Statistical Manual of Mental Disorders*, Third Edition, Washington DC: APA.

Barcroft, J., Hunt, G.H. and Dufton, D. (1918). *Reports of the Chemical Warfare Committee*, No. 9, *Treatment*. PRO, WO142/103.

Boyd, J.S.K. (1938). Active immunization against tetanus, *Journal of the Royal Army Medical Corps*, 70, 289–307.

Cantor, D. (2000). The diseased body, in R. Cooter and J. Pickstone (Eds), *Companion to Medicine in the Twentieth Century*, London: Routledge, pp. 347–66.

Christophers, A.J. (1997). The epidemic of heart disease amongst British soldiers during the First World War, *War and Society*, 15, 53–72.

Clark, J.M. (1931). *The Costs of the World War to the American People*, New Haven: Yale University Press.

Cummins, S.L. and Elliott, T.R. (1916). Notes on reports dealing with cardiac disabilities as the results of drift gas poisoning, 19 November. PRO, WO142/106.

Da Costa, J.M. (1871). On irritable heart: a clinical study of a form of functional cardiac disorder and its consequences, *American Journal of Medical Sciences*, **121**, 17–52.

Dean, C.G.T. (1950). *The Royal Hospital Chelsea*, London: Hutchinson.

Dean, E.T. (1997). *Shook over Hell, Post-Traumatic Stress, Vietnam and the Civil War*. Cambridge Massachusetts: Harvard University Press.

Douglas, C.G. (1918a). *Note on Invaliding Factors amongst Casualties*, 10 January 1918. PRO, WO142/102.

Douglas, C.G. (1918b). *Memo to Edkins*, 14 April 1918. PRO, WO142/104.

Douglas, C.G. (1918c). *Memo to W. Pasteur*, 28 March 1918. PRO, WO142/106.

Durbach, N. (2005). *Bodily Matters, The Anti-Vaccination Movement in England 1853–1907*. Durham: Duke University Press.

Elliott, T.R. (1918). Memo, 21 September 1918. PRO, WO142/104.

Elliott, T.R. and Douglas, C.G. (1916). A report on the casualties due to gas poisoning, December 1915 to August 1916. PRO, WO142/102, p.13.

Elliot Smith, G. (1916). Shock and the soldier, *Lancet*, i, 813–17.

French, D. (2000). *Raising Churchill's Army: The British Army and the War against Germany 1919–1945*, Oxford: Oxford University Press.

Glass, A.J. (1973). Lessons learned, in A.J. Glass (Ed.) *Neuropsychiatry in World War II*, Volume 2, *Overseas Theaters*, Washington DC: Office of the Surgeon General, US Army, pp. 989–1027.

Grinker, R.R. and Spiegel, J.P. (1945). *Men Under Stress*, London: J. & A. Churchill.

Haldane, J.S. (1917). The therapeutic administration of oxygen, *British Medical Journal*, 1917, **1**, 181–83.

Haldane, J.S., Meakins, J.C. and Priestley, J.G. (1918), *Investigations of Chronic Cases of Gas Poisoning on Behalf of the Medical Research Committee*. PRO, WO142/106. 1. Oxygen therapy was used to treat chronic cases characterised by the symptoms of disordered action of the heart (DAH), namely palpitations, rapid or irregular heart beat, chest pain and shortness of breath, observation having suggested that these were the result of frequent but excessively shallow breathing.

Harrison, M. (2004). *Medicine and Victory, British Military Medicine in the Second World War*, Oxford: Oxford University Press.

Hyams, K.C., Wignall, F.S. and Roswell, R. (1996). War syndromes and their evaluation: from the US Civil War to the Persian Gulf War, *Annals of Internal Medicine*, **125**, 398–405.

James, G.W.B. (1955). Narrative, Resume, Comments and Conclusions concerning the Middle East Force from September 1940 to July 1943 (typescript).

Jones, E. (2006). LMF; the use of psychiatric stigma in the Royal Air Force during the Second World War, *Journal of Military History*, **70**, 439–58.

Jones, E. and Wessely, S. (2001). The origins of British military psychiatry before the First World War, *War and Society*, **24**, 91–108.

Jones, E., and Wessely, S. (2005). War syndromes: the impact of culture on medically unexplained symptoms. *Medical History*, **49**, 55–78.

Jones, E., Hodgins Vermaas, R., McCartney, H., Everitt, B., Beech, B., Poynter, D., Palmer, I., Hyams, K., and Wessely, S. (2002). Post-combat syndromes from the Boer War to the Gulf: a cluster analysis of their nature and attribution. *British Medical Journal*, **324**, 321–24.

Jones, E., Hodgins Vermaas, R., Beech, C., Palmer, I. Hyams, K. and Wessely, S. (2003a). Mortality and post-combat syndromes: UK veterans of the Boer War and World War One, *Military Medicine*, **168**, 414–418.

Kilshaw, S.M. (2004), Friendly fire, The construction of Gulf War syndrome, *Anthropology and Medicine*, **11**, 149–60.

Langman, M.J.S. (1979). *The Epidemiology of Chronic Digestive Disease*, London: Edward Arnold.

Latcham, A.P. (1997). 'Journey's End': Ex-servicemen and the state during and after the Great War. DPhil thesis, Oxford University.

Lee, H.A., Gabriel, R., Bolton, J.P.G., Bale, A.J. and Blatchley, N.F. (2001). Clinical findings of the second 1000 UK Gulf War veterans who attended the Ministry of Defence's Medical Assessment Programme, *Journal of the Royal Army Medical Corps*, **147**, 153–60.

Lee, H.A., Gabriel, R., Bolton, J.P.G., Bale, A.J. and Jackson M. (2002). Health status and clinical diagnoses of 3000 Gulf War veterans, *Journal of the Royal Society of Medicine*, **95**, 491–97.

Leese, P. (2002). *Shell Shock, Traumatic Neuroses and the British Soldiers of the First World War*, Houndmills, Basingstoke: Palgrave Macmillan.

Levine, S.A. (1965). The origin of the term neurocirculatory asthenia, *New England Journal of Medicine*, **273**, 604–05.

Lewis T. (1917). *Report upon Soldiers Returned as Cases of 'Disordered Action of the Heart' (DAH) or 'Valvular Disease of the Heart' (VDH)*. London: Medical Research Committee.

Lewis, T. (1918). The tolerance of physical exertion, as shown by soldiers suffering from so-called 'irritable heart', *British Medical Journal*, **1**, 363–65.

Lindsay, M. (2000). *So Few Got Through*, London: Leo Cooper.

Lister, W.J. (1918). Report on the effects on the eyes of irritant gases, 14 October 1918. PRO, WO142/107.

Mackenzie, J. (1916). The soldier's heart, *British Medical Journal*, **1**, 117–19.

Mackenzie, J. (1920). A lecture on the soldier's heart and war neurosis: a study of symptomatology, *British Medical Journal*, **1**, 530–34.

Maclean, W.C. (1864). The influence of the present knapsack and accoutrements on the health of the infantry soldier, *Journal of the Royal United Service Institution*, **8**, 105–15.

Mitchell, T.J. and Smith, G.M. (1931). *Medical Services, Casualties and Medical Statistics of the Great War*, London: HMSO.

Mott, F.W. (1916a). Special discussion on shellshock without visible signs of injury. *Proceedings of the Royal Society of Medicine*, **9**, i–xxiv.

Mott, F.W. (1916b). The effects of high explosives upon the central nervous system. *Lancet*, i, 331–8; 441–9.

Mott, F.W. (1919). *War Neuroses and Shellshock*. London: Henry Froude and Hodder & Stoughton.

Moulin, A.M. (2000). The defended body, in R. Cooter and J. Pickstone (Eds), *Companion to Medicine in the Twentieth Century*, London: Routledge, pp. 385–98.

Myers, C.S. (1915). A contribution to the study of shellshock, *Lancet*, i, 316–20.

Myers, C.S. (1916). Contributions to the study of shellshock, being an account of certain cases treated by hypnosis, *Lancet*, i, 65–69.

Myers, C.S. (1940). *Shellshock in France 1914–18, Based on a War Diary* Cambridge: Cambridge University Press.

Oppenheimer, B.S. (1942). Neurocirculatory asthenia and related problems in military medicine. *Bulletin of the New York Academy of Medicine*, 18, 367–82.

Sargant, W. (1967). *The Unquiet Mind, The Autobiography of a Physician in Psychological Medicine*, London: Heinemann.

Sheffield, G. (2001). *Forgotten Victory, The First World War: Myths and Realities*, London: Headline.

Shephard, B. (1996). The early treatment of mental disorders: R.G. Rows and Maghull 1914–1918, in H. Freeman and G.E. Berrios (Eds) *150 Years of British Psychiatry*, Volume 2, *The Aftermath*, London: Gaskell, pp. 434–64.

Shephard, B. (1999). 'Pitiless psychology': the role of prevention in British military psychiatry in the Second World War, *History of Psychiatry*, 10, 491–542.

Shephard, B. (2000). *A War of Nerves, Soldiers and Psychiatrists, 1914–1991*. London: Jonathan Cape.

Sloggett, A.T. (1916). *Memorandum on Gas Poisoning*, London: HMSO (PRO, WO142/101).

Southborough, Lord (1922). *Report of the War Office Committee of Enquiry into 'Shell-shock'*, London: HMSO.

Stafford-Clark, D. (nd). Bomber command and Lack of Moral Fibre (typescript).

Strachan, H. (2003). *The First World War A New Illustrated History*, London: Simon & Schuster.

Symonds, C.P. (1943a). Anxiety neurosis in combatants, *Lancet*, ii, 785–89.

Symonds, C.P. (1943b). The human response to flying stress, *British Medical Journal*, 2, 703–6; 740–4.

Tidy, H.L. (1941). Discussion on dyspepsia in the armed forces, *Proceedings of the Royal Society of Medicine*, 34, 413–14.

Tidy, H.L. (1943). Peptic ulcer and dyspepsia in the army, *British Medical Journal*, 2, 473–7.

Unwin, C., Blatchley, N., Coker, W., Ferry, S., Hotopf, M., Hull, L., Ismail, K., Palmer, I., David., A. and Wessely, S. (1999). Health of UK servicemen who served in Persian Gulf War, *Lancet*, 353: 169–78.

Venning, J. A. (1919). The etiology of disordered action of the heart, a report on 7803 cases, *British Medical Journal*, 2, 337–39.

Walker, M. (2005). Transforming the UK Armed Forces, *Royal United Service Institute Journal*, 150, 45–48.

Ward, S. R. E. (1975). *The War Generation, Veterans of the First World* War, Port Washington, NY: Kennikat Press.

Wessely, S. (1991). History of postviral fatigue syndrome, *British Medical Bulletin*, 47, 919–41.

Wilson, W.D. (1904). *Report on the Medical Arrangements in the South African War*, London: HMSO.

Wood, P. (1941a). Da Costa's syndrome (or effort syndrome), *British Medical Journal*, 1, 767–72.

Wood, P. (1941b). Da Costa's Syndrome (or effort syndrome), The mechanism of the somatic manifestation, *British Medical Journal*, 1, 805–11.

Wood, P. (1941c). Aetiology of Da Costa's syndrome, *British Medical Journal*, 1, 845–51.

Wooley, C.F. (1982). Jacob Mendez DaCosta: medical teacher, clinician and clinical investigator, *American Journal of Cardiology*, 50, 1145–48.

Wooley, C.F. (1986). 'From irritable heart to mitral valve prolapse: World War I, the British experience and James Mackenzie', *American Journal of Cardiology*, 57, 463–66.

Wooley, C.F. (2002). *The Irritable Heart of Soldiers and the Origins of Anglo-American Cardiology: The US Civil War (1861) to World War One (1918)*, Aldershot: Ashgate Publishing.

Wootton, G. (1956). *The Official History of the British Legion*, London: Macdonald & Evans.

Wootton, G. (1963). *The Politics of Influence, British Ex-servicemen, Cabinet Decisions and Cultural Change (1917–57)*, London: Routledge.

Young, A. (1995). *The Harmony of Illusions, Inventing Post-Traumatic Stress Disorder*, Princeton, New Jersey: Princeton University Press.

# 3

# Causation

Harry Lee

## INTRODUCTION

Ever since the Gulf War of 1990–91 (Op Granby) there has been a demand from certain veterans' activist groups for ever more research to be undertaken on so-called 'Gulf War syndrome'. The first media report of 'Gulf War syndrome' appeared in the US in early 1993. The seminal work of Unwin et al. (1999) showed that Gulf veterans reported more symptoms than did comparison groups, but could not identify a single or specific causative factor. In a further evaluation of their findings, Ismail et al. (1999) could not find any evidence to support the existence of a unique Gulf War Syndrome. Murphy (1999), reviewing the available evidence, acknowledged that there probably was no specific syndrome, but concluded that personnel do suffer after most wars. Murphy also noted, as did Hyams et al. (1996), that poorly defined post-war illnesses have occurred after each major conflict of the Twentieth century.

Now, some 14 years on, no specific aetiology has been found and the likelihood of so doing diminishes the further we are in time from the original conflict. Many studies have been based on recall questionnaires, and this technique has been seriously questioned by McCauley et al. (1999a, b) and Hotopf and Wessely (2005). Sen (2002) warned of the severe limitations of self-reported morbidity and how very misleading such data can be. Observation must always be better than self-report. It has been reported that veterans claim exposures that they can be

*War and Health: Lessons from the Gulf War*  Edited by Harry Lee & Edgar Jones
© 2007 John Wiley & Sons, Ltd

proved never to have received or experienced (Greenberg *et al.*, 2004). Thus claims are made of 14 or more vaccinations in a day, soldiers having taken four or more NAPS (pyridostigmine bromide) tablets a day, or hearing positive chemical alarms going off at, say, Al Jubayl in January 1991. In addition, there are those who believe that they were subjected to significant cyclosarin fallout as a result of the Khamisayah dump explosions in March 1991 when they were never near the location (MoD, 2005b). Others believe they were experimented upon with pyridostigmine bromide, a drug used in clinical practice since 1935 with a remarkably good track record. Furthermore, in 2000, as a result of considerable, oft times irresponsible, media coverage, the depleted uranium scare was launched, leading to the development of the Depleted Uranium Oversight Board in 2002. Some researchers have favoured a *Mycoplasma fermentans* theory (Nicholson, 1996), and others (Asa *et al.*, 2000) squalene contamination of vaccines as the cause of veterans' ill health. Yet others claimed it was not just individual exposures, but a combination that caused specific illnesses. How well founded are these hypotheses?

In a small but carefully controlled study, Spencer *et al.* (2001) showed that unexplained illness associated with the Gulf War is particularly associated with combat conditions, heat stress and having sought medical attention during the Gulf War. When they controlled the study for multiple simultaneous exposures during the Gulf War, interactions around pyridostigmine bromide, insecticides and insect repellents, and heat stress, these were not found to be significant. They concluded from their results that most unexplained illness in Gulf War veterans could not be explained by neurotoxic effects of exposure to chemicals that inhibit cholinesterase activity.

# POSSIBLE CAUSES OF GULF WAR SYNDROME

## Mycoplasma Fermentans

*Mycoplasma fermentans* has been postulated as a possible cause of specific Gulf War illness (Nicholson and Nicholson, 1996; Nicholson, 1996). They suggested that Gulf veterans were particularly exposed to this protozoon, resulting in vague ill health. As a result of their claims, the Department of Defense (DoD, USA) undertook a one-year randomised, double-blind, placebo-controlled, trial by treating veterans with doxycycline. No improvement in the health status was noted at 1 year in this trial (Donta *et al.*, 2004). Perhaps this result was not surprising since previously Lo *et al.* (2000) had not found any serological evidence to suggest that infection with *M. fermentans* was associated with the development of 'Gulf War illness'. Furthermore, routine testing for *Mycoplasma fermentans* has never been undertaken in the UK and has since been dropped in the USA.

Nevertheless, it is perhaps worth recording that soon after many veterans returned home from the Gulf, some were treated by the public as if they had a dangerous communicable disease. Some journalists resorted to wearing gloves, gowns and masks when interviewing them, some veterans' children were not allowed into school, and regrettably some veterans were shunned.

## Leishmaniasis

Leishmaniasis was another early theory for an acquired desert illness causing long-term ill health in Gulf veterans (Magill *et al.* 1993). There had been such concern that the US DoD (November 1991) banned blood donation by US Service personnel who had served in the Gulf War. However, as a result of so few cases being detected, the DoD lifted this ban in January 1993. When Joseph (1997) published his report no further cases had been reported since the original 12 identified. No such case was found in the UK deployed force and testing for leishmaniasis A and B was dropped in 2000 (Lee *et al.*, 2002). In fact, infectious diseases were not a major cause of ill health or loss of manpower during the Gulf conflict (Hyams *et al.*, 1995). The most commonly reported infectious diseases during deployment were mild acute diarrhoea cases and upper respiratory tract infections.

## Squalene

Squalene was suggested by Asa *et al.* (2000) as a cause for autoimmune-type diseases in Gulf veterans. Her methodology was found to be seriously flawed, as a result of which further research in that area was not funded or supported by the DoD/VA USA (Laforce and Diniega, 2000). Squalene was never a component of any vaccine used in vaccination programmes for UK servicemen going to the Gulf. Incidentally, squalene is a normal constituent of human sebum.

## Vaccinations

There have been many claims about the role of vaccinations in causing long term ill health amongst veterans. It has been alleged that a large number of vaccinations, up to 14, were given on any one day to veterans (according only to veteran recall) during Op Granby. However, these claims are based on individual reports and no objective evidence has been produced to verify these assertions (Greenberg *et al.*, 2004). The vaccination programme of 1990–91 was not carried out as well as it might have been, poor risk communication and record keeping having been particular problems. Nevertheless all vaccines used were properly licensed. There is no doubt that some veterans experienced acute reactions to their anthrax and/or plague vaccinations, and a few were casevaced out of theatre.

Rook and Zumla (1997) published a hypothetical paper suggesting that multiple vaccines given to Service personnel during the Gulf conflict might be responsible for the so-called 'Gulf War syndrome' by altering the cytokine $Th^1/Th^2$ balance. Then Unwin *et al.* (1999), in a study on veterans reporting 6 years after their participation in the Persian Gulf War, found that veterans who may have been given multiple vaccinations were more likely to report illnesses with multiple symptoms. This suggestion was further explored by Hotopf *et al.* (2000), but their results were somewhat conflicting and did not support the Rook and Zumla hypothesis.

In the Hotopf study, more than 20 types of exposure were implicated but not checked against controls. For example, they found that post-traumatic stress disorder was related to multiple vaccinations given before deployment and not during. Of 3284 respondents in this study who kept vaccination records, 923 (28 %) appeared to suggest that there was an apparent interaction between multiple vaccines and deployment. However, this finding could have resulted from a restricted sample combined with self-report bias. For example, anthrax vaccination was reported much more frequently than pertussis vaccination, when in fact they had been given concomitantly. Since MOD records suggest that pertussis vaccination records were reasonably accurate, it is probable that anthrax vaccination was over-reported. Self-report questionnaires completed long after the event carry a real risk that symptomatic veterans who had kept their vaccination records might have been aware of the hypothesis being tested and hence over-reported the vaccinations they received during deployment. McManus (1997) had written in the *Sunday Times* in June that veterans could get compensation if the Rook and Zumla hypothesis was confirmed. However, the Hotopf paper did not demonstrate that vaccinations were related to increased eczema or psoriasis problems, and they found no association between multiple vaccinations and hay fever, and indeed little support, if any, for the existence of a unique 'Gulf War syndrome'. This paper was also strongly criticised by Bolton *et al.* (2001) who found flaws in their methodology and suggested that the only conclusion from their work was that there is a weak association between multiple immunisations and illness in Gulf veterans. Likewise, Gray *et al.* (2002) studied self-reported symptoms and medical conditions amongst 11 868 Gulf War/era veterans – Seabee health study (68.6 % response rate). This study showed that the data did not support a specific aetiologic exposure during Gulf War service, but did demonstrate a strong association and high prevalence of self-reported, multi-symptom, conditions in a large group of symptomatic Gulf War veterans.

Also, Upshall (2000), in a historical review about possible toxic exposures during Op Granby 1990–1 found no evidence to support a unique 'Gulf War syndrome'. Neither could he find a single hypothesis then, as now, that had supporting scientifically robust evidence to explain the aetiology of health concerns amongst Gulf War veterans. Shaheen (2000) could not find any conclusive evidence that multiple vaccinations during deployment were to blame for veterans' ill health. He did, however, make the important observation that better record keeping in the future would best help evaluating post-conflict health concerns of veterans.

In a controlled study, Enstone *et al.* (2003) studied adverse medical outcomes in RAF personnel at five different bases following anthrax vaccinations. Mild side effects were noted in 11 % of cases, but no serious side effects were observed. Interestingly, they found that the RAF base at which the personnel were located not only had a significant impact on whether anthrax vaccination was accepted, but also on the frequency of reported side effects.

However, there is no evidence to show that long-term health problems have resulted in animals from the vaccination programme used during Op Granby. The vaccination interactions programme carried out at Porton Down initially used guinea pig models (Griffiths *et al.*, 2001). These were comprehensive, in-depth, studies investigating the effects of multiple vaccines and pyridostigmine in these animals on haematological, biochemical, immunological and endocrinological systems, and general health consequences. Apart from slight pyrexia and insignificant weight loss, no abnormalities were detected and the animals remained healthy. The guinea pig model is considered preferable to the mouse model, for the latter is known to have a low sensitivity to anthrax vaccine and a high sensitivity to pertussis vaccine, the reverse of the human situation. In another study using the mouse model, the effects of pertussis vaccine, anthrax vaccine, vaccine combinations and aluminium salts were studied (Rijpkema *et al.*, 2005). They found that pertussis vaccines, vaccine combinations and aluminium salts caused illness, splenomegaly and significant weight loss, whilst inoculation of anthrax vaccine caused little effect. However, the authors emphasised the need for a very cautious interpretation of these results, bearing in mind how the host model is very different to the human recipient of such vaccines.

In further studies, Dstl Porton Down, investigating the effects of vaccine combinations with or without pyridostigmine bromide, the marmoset model was chosen as being more representative of the human species. In this investigation, immunological, biochemical, endocrino-logical, muscle function, neurocognitive behaviour, sleep patterns, EEG responses, general health and body weight were observed. At 3 months no adverse immunological responses in particular had been shown, nor any untoward effects in other parameters measured. Further follow-up at 12 months (Stevens *et al.*, 2006; Williams *et al.*, 2006) have shown virtually identical results. This is strong evidence against the long-term ill-health effects described by some Gulf War veterans being caused by vaccinations.

Nevertheless, lessons were learnt from Op Granby, so that by the time of Op Telic 2003, only anthrax vaccination was offered on an informed consent basis, without the adjuvant pertussis, and plague was no longer given. This resulted from good clinical-evidence-based medicine.

After Op Telic, there was speculation in some parts of the media that anthrax vaccinations were associated with a cluster of birth defects. This was not substantiated. Furthermore, the UK Health Protection Agency (2005) has robustly repudiated any connection between anthrax vaccinations and birth defects.

## Pyridostigmine Bromide

Pyridostigmine bromide (PB) was issued as NAPS (nerve agent pre-treatment set) to servicemen deployed to the Gulf. Just before, or at the onset, of the air war (January 15/16, 1991), personnel were instructed to take PB, 30 mg, 8 hourly, and this was carefully observed amongst most UK units. Some Servicemen did not persevere with PB, with which they should have continued until 28 February 1991, the end of ground war, because of side effects, for example, urinary frequency, bowel disturbances, or lack of conviction about the efficacy of this agent. At the Gulf Veterans' Medical Assessment Programme (GVMAP), there are only one or two records of individuals taking more PB than recommended or for a longer period.

In some quarters, PB has been targeted as being the real culprit of Gulf War illnesses. This arose in particular from the speculation by Haley and Kurt (1997) of 'severe neurological damage' in a small, uncontrolled subset of Seabees. They suggested that PB and other toxic agents, such as organophosphates, DEET (N, N-diethyl-m-toluamide), all known to have been used to different degrees during Op Granby (Haley et al., 1997) might be responsible for ill-health amongst veterans. These hypotheses were also based on self-reported exposure to neurotoxic chemical combinations during the Gulf War.

Friedman et al. (1996) suggested that giving PB in a stressful environment of conflict could facilitate the passage of PB, a quaternary cholinesterase inhibitor, across the blood/brain barrier, thus enhancing neuronal excitability and inducing early immediate transcriptual responses. The investigators exposed mice to relatively mild stress, that is swimming in cold water, and concluded that the blood/brain barrier was breached in this setting and reported a stress induced increase in brain cholinesterase inhibition in pyridostigmine-treated mice. These were unexpected findings, and have not been replicated (Lallement et al., 1998). Grauer et al. (2000) undertook further studies, which were carefully controlled, of swim-stressed mice and looked at brain cholinesterase activities. They found that PB had no effect on central cholinesterase activity in any of the parameters measured (gender, age and strain). In particular, they did not find that stress exposure altered pyridostigmine effect on brain cholinesterase (CHE) activity. They did not find any changes in blood/brain barrier permeability during stress.

Other studies (Griffiths et al., 2001) have examined the biological consequences of multiple vaccines and pyridostigmine pre-treatment given concomitantly in the guinea pig model (see above). The animals in these studies remained generally healthy and active without visible adverse signs throughout the study.

This same group (Stevens et al., 2006; Williams et al., 2006) carried out similar studies on marmosets following co-administration of multiple vaccines and PB. In this exhaustive study, the preliminary results did not indicate there were any adverse immune consequences at

0–3 months following vaccination and/or PB administration, and these findings have been upheld in their final report

Chaney *et al.* (2000) studied the acute effects of an insect repellent, DEET, on cholinesterase inhibition induced by PB in rats. Their research was prompted following reports by Abou-Donia *et al.* (1996), who reported the results of experiments on hens, which showed an increase in neurotoxic effects following concurrent exposure to DEET and PB. They found, unlike Abou-Donia *et al.*, that DEET did not alter PB-induced inhibition of CHE activity in rat diaphragm, heart or blood. They also found that administration of DEET alone had no effect on CHE activity, and that PB alone did not inhibit CHE in the whole brain, but that PB plus DEET caused significant inhibition of whole-brain CHE activity to approximately 66 % of control. Nevertheless, they concluded that it was unlikely that lethal interaction between PB and DEET is mediated through a cholinergic effect resulting from increased inhibition of CHE.

Kant *et al.* (2001) studied the combined effects of PB and chronic stress on brain cortical and blood acetyl cholinesterase, corticosterone, prolactin and alternation performance in rats. They concluded that PB does not exacerbate the effects of stress on performance or levels of stress hormones. Their data did not suggest that stress enables PB to cross the blood/brain barrier.

There is, therefore, a considerable body of evidence refuting the idea that PB alone or in combination with other agents is the cause of any specific Gulf War illness. The suggestion by Friedman *et al.* (1996) that PB in a stress environment causes increased permeability of the blood/brain barrier has never been confirmed. It must be remembered that the prophylactic dose used in Gulf War veterans was 30 mg tds, well below the therapeutic range recommended in the British National Formulary (2004). Furthermore, many veterans who experienced immediate side effects as a result of taking PB stopped taking the tablets. The dose taken was not only low but only over a short period of time. For example, Bale and Lee (2005) found only a very small number of veterans whose symptoms (bladder – detrusor muscle instability, or intestinal – onset of irritable bowel symptoms) could be temporally related to the ingestion of PB.

## Khamisayah Arms Dump Explosions, March 1991

This topic has been the subject of intensive investigations by the DoD (USA) (Winkenwerder, 2002). No such investigations have been undertaken in the UK, as it was thought unnecessary to duplicate American studies. It has been estimated that some 321 kg of sarin and cyclosarin were released from the demolitions at the Khamisayah arms pit, and another 51 kg from bunker 73. However, there is no published evidence to show that any UK or US service personnel suffered adverse acute health effects from any such potential exposure (MoD, 2005).

Epidemiological studies in the US (Smith *et al.* 2003; 2004) have not found any association between deployment within the estimated Khamisayah exposure area and the subsequent development of ill health. One observation by Smith *et al.* (2003) suggested that personnel possibly exposed to sub-clinical doses of nerve agents might be at increased risk for hospital admission as a result of circulatory disorders, particularly cardiac dysrhythmias. The increase was very small and inconclusive, but merits further evaluation. No excess cardiovascular disease amongst Gulf veterans was observed by Bale and Lee (2005).

No UK armed forces were involved in the Khamisayah demolitions (MoD website, 2005b). The nearest unit was some 130 km away from the Khamisayah event and would not therefore have been exposed to the highest possible levels of nerve agent present only in the immediate vicinity of the explosions. However, the MoD (MoD website, 2005b), on the basis of the DoD 2002 plume model, has estimated that almost 9000 UK personnel were located within the possible area. Nevertheless, taking into account all the available evidence regarding neurotoxicity of the agents, where personnel may have been deployed, and duration of any potential exposure, the MoD concluded that there was a remote possibility that there could have been exposure to a very low level of nerve agent. However, it must be emphasised that any such exposure would have been minuscule and of short duration (below a critical level or duration based on current knowledge), insufficient to have any biologically detectable effect, cause any immediate ill-health effects, or be related to any of the later symptoms of ill health that some veterans complain of.

## Depleted Uranium

Depleted uranium (DU) munitions were used for the first time in battle during Op Granby, when both US and UK military forces fired them. However, a great amount of research has not shown that any veterans experienced acute immediate health effects as a result of potential exposure to DU (be that radioactive or the heavy metal effect), and there is no evidence to support any long-term ill-health effects from alleged or actual (retained DU fragments) DU exposure.

DU is 40 % less radioactive than naturally occurring uranium, but shares the same heavy metal effects. DU is weakly radioactive and emits three types of ionising radiation: $\alpha$ and $\beta$ particles, and photons (gamma rays and X-rays). When a DU munition hits metal plating, immense heat is generated and penetration occurs whilst, simultaneously, a localised small cloud of dust containing DU particles is generated. In turn, exposure effects depend upon whether DU is internal or external to the body. DU gains entry into the body either by inhalation or ingestion, and additionally there is radiation exposure, mainly from $\beta$ particles by direct contact with the skin. Only DU particles of less than 5 $\mu$m in diameter gain access to the pulmonary alveoli. Thus the majority of inhaled particles are rapidly cleared in mucus, or are swallowed and excreted. Some uranium particles from the pulmonary alveoli or gastrointestinal tract are absorbed into the blood stream and rapidly excreted by the kidneys, the main target organ for any adverse DU effects. Therefore, if small particles remain in the pulmonary alveoli some of them may be cleared in the bronchial tree or conveyed to local lymph nodes. Lymph nodes are less DU radio sensitive than is pulmonary tissue.

It was never the policy of GVMAP to test routinely for urinary uranium (the phrase used then was 'depleted uranium') in veterans attending this department. However, because of the intense public and media driven interest in 1999, GVMAP offered a pilot study on depleted uranium urinary tests to Gulf War veterans who would be admitted to a metabolic unit so that a 24-hour urine sample could be collected and then divided into three aliquots to be analysed by quality controlled laboratories, two chosen by MoD (GVMAP) and one by the veterans. In the event, the most vociferous group, NGVFA, decided not to cooperate with such an initiative, which had received tri-Service ethical committee clearance.

Lee *et al.* (2001) addressed the question as to whether or not depleted uranium was really a health issue amongst Gulf War veterans. They concluded that it was not. More importantly, McDiarmid (2001), whilst recognising that depleted uranium munitions were used for the first time in Gulf War 1990–91, also noted that there was a sizeable store of knowledge that had been gathered over the past 50 years with respect to studies of uranium miners, millers and other processors worldwide. Her view was that there was no evidence to suggest that uranium caused an increase in lung cancer, or lymphatic and bone malignancies. This review acknowledged concerns about possible connections between DU and ill health, but found no compelling evidence in support. With respect to non-cancer health effects and thereby referring to Gulf War illnesses, the important comment was made: 'There is still no single candidate hazard which serves as a unifying explanation, depleted uranium included'. As McDiarmid asserted: 'it is uncommon to have the benefit of 50 years of human epidemiological evidence in managing any of the environmental occupational public health problems facing the global medical community today'. Nevertheless, in spite of these reports, the MoD (2002), persuaded by recommendations from the Royal Society, decided to set up the Depleted Uranium Oversight Board, which in turn implemented a screening programme whereby veterans could be tested on demand for urinary DU in quality controlled laboratories. Interestingly, by 2005, only some 104 + 32 (the latter in their pilot study) veterans had availed themselves of this opportunity and all tests thus far have been negative (DUOB 2005). This outcome would have been anticipated from the reviews by Lee *et al.* (2001) and McDiarmid *et al.* (2001).

In a separate MoD monitoring programme (2002) where veterans of Op Telic (2003) can also be tested for DU, only 350 personnel have come forward and all have tested negative except for those with retained DU shrapnel fragments. Such results cast doubt on having dedicated DU screening programmes. In any case, there is no therapeutic strategy available for those who are found to have high urinary uranium concentrations.

An interesting study (Greenberg *et al.*, 2004) studied the characteristics of those service personnel, who, as a result of the screening test set up by the Depleted Uranium Oversight Board of the MoD (DUOB), might avail themselves of urinary DU screening. In their questionnaire survey, 2192 responded on the issue of DU screening (92 %). Of the responders, 529 (24.4 %) reported a desire for DU screening. They tended to be significantly younger than those who did not want screening and it was noted that there was significant gender difference, a positive response given by 28 % of servicemen and 100 % of servicewomen. Personnel from the Army and Royal Navy had higher rates of positive responses, but there were no differences in the rates between those still serving and those discharged from the services. Again, as might be expected from previous studies, the officers had a significantly lower rate of positive uptake than did NCOs and lower ranks. This study looked at veterans from both Gulf (1990–91) and Bosnia deployments. The belief that one was suffering from 'Gulf War syndrome' was also significantly associated with wanting a DU screening test. There were limitations to this study inasmuch as it was weighted to make up a sample, which was over representative of fatigued individuals and, therefore, overall levels of psychopathology found were generally greater than would be expected in a random sample of military population. The conclusion of the study was that DU screening is primarily determined by current health status rather than by a proxy measure of risk exposure. Nevertheless, it is noted that those who desire DU screening recount more DU exposure by retrospective self-report. Somewhat surprisingly, Greenberg *et al.* (2004) deduced from their study, which indicated that 529 would like to be screened for DU, then 12 720 personnel would want DU screening based on a simple extrapolation of the 53 549 deployed on Op Granby. Taking into consideration Balkan deployment, they also suggested that a further 24 000 may want screening, making in all almost 37 000. However, this is simply not borne out by the findings of the DUOB screening programme. This is another example of where extrapolation from self-reported questionnaires can lead to over-exaggerated responses about certain (i.e. DU) exposures, and regrettably to conclusions that may lead to very expensive experimental protocols with virtually no value to any veteran concerned. The DUOB screening programme closed in January 2006 through lack of ongoing interest by the veteran community.

Furthermore, screening programmes should not be undertaken lightly, for they must also take account of social and psychological costs (Stewart-Brown and Farmer, 1997); thus for prostate cancer there is no evidence that early treatment improves outcome. There is also the problem of false positive results. Lee *et al.* (2005) also advocated a very cautious approach to screening programmes and to over-investigating veterans unless there are clear-cut clinical indications.

Gulf War 1 veterans in the US, concerned about past exposure to DU, have been offered biologic monitoring for total urinary uranium by the Departments of Veterans' Affairs and Defense since the late 1990s (McDiarmid *et al.*, 2004). Two hundred and twenty-seven veterans submitted 24-hour urine samples for analysis between January 2000 and December 2002, and completed questionnaires describing their wartime exposures. Twenty-two veterans showed urinary uranium concentrations in the high range. Isotope analyses available for 21 out of these 22 revealed that all but three of these samples contained natural but not depleted uranium. The three in question had retained DU shrapnel as a result of their past injuries. The study suggested that elevated urine uranium values in the absence of retained DU fragments are unlikely, which mirrors the UK experience.

Another study (McDiarmid *et al.*, 2000) investigated 60 US Gulf veterans who were victims of friendly fire with depleted uranium munitions, of which 15 had retained metal fragments of DU in soft tissue and continued to excrete markedly raised urinary uranium concentrations. None of these veterans had developed leukaemia, bone or lung cancer. This study evaluated the potential clinical health effects of DU exposure of Gulf War veterans compared to non-exposed Gulf War veterans. History and a follow-up medical examination were carried out on 29 exposed veterans and 38 non-exposed. Outcome measures included urinary uranium concentrations, clinical laboratory values and psychiatric and neuro-cognitive assessment. Not surprisingly, DU exposed Gulf War veterans with retained metal shrapnel fragments were still excreting high urinary concentrations 7 years after exposure. Adverse effects on the kidney (the prime target organ) were not found. Neurocognitive examinations demonstrated a statistical relationship between urinary uranium concentrations and lowered performance on computerized tests assessing performance efficiency. In addition, elevated urinary uranium was statistically related to high prolactin concentrations. The conclusions were, however, that effects related to retained metal fragments associated with high urinary uranium concentrations were of a subtle nature, i.e. subtle perturbations in the reproductive and central nervous systems without any general ill-health effects.

The kidney is the main target organ for any acute DU effects arising from high dose exposures, whilst the skeleton is the main repository for DU. Nevertheless, slow release over the years from bone DU reservoirs still makes the kidney the main target, particularly the proximal tubule epithelium for chemical and, less so, radiation effects. Murray *et al.* (2002) were of the view that health hazards from DU munitions on the battlefield are unlikely to cause any measurable excesses of cancers. This view is strongly supported by Bolton and Foster (2002) who found no evidence either of increased all-cause or cause-specific mortality due to exposure to uranium (occupationally exposed groups and case reports of accidental acute chronic exposure) or even increased prevalence of diseases attributable to uranium amongst the exposed. This is supported by the DASA six monthly reviews (DASA, 2006). Thus, Murray *et al.* remind us that the hazards of DU munitions should be kept in perspective, and that any prospective studies will have to be carefully controlled, and take into account changes of renal function with age, and cancer-risk-compounding factors such as smoking, nature of occupation, and other medical conditions.

Similarly, at GVMAP, no recognised ill-health effects have been seen as a result of possible DU exposure. This includes no immediate effects (radiation or heavy metal) reported by veterans, or long-term ill-health concerns that could possibly be related to either heavy metal or radiation effects (Lee *et al.*, 2002; Bale and Lee, 2005). Although many provocative and indeed prominent statements have been made by various pressure groups on both sides of the Atlantic, there is no scientific evidence to support the claim that ill health amongst Gulf War veterans is due to DU exposure. Similar observations have been made elsewhere (Lee *et al.*, 2001).

## Smoke and Fumes from Burning Oil Wells

No one doubts the ferocity of oil-well fires and their dramatic effects on the local environment. Many veterans have said that day was virtually turned into night and many seen at GVMAP had photographs to prove the point. However, the US was particularly quick in testing air samples at the time (Heller, 1992), and found no increased pollutant contamination in the smoky atmosphere. The darkness was caused by carbon particles or their coating of silicone particles, but considering other potential pollutants such as carbon monoxide, benzene, toluene, ethyl benzene, xylenes, sulfurous or nitrous fumes, they were no more concentrated than in major busy US or Western European cities, strangulated by an ever increasing number of motor vehicles (US Army Environmental Hygiene Agency, 1991 ).

Later, Smith *et al.* (2002a) addressed the issue of whether or not exposure to smoke and fumes from the Kuwaiti oil well fires resulted in long term ill health amongst veterans. They were able to study complete exposure and demographic data on 405 142 active-duty Gulf War veterans who did not remain in the region after the war. The authors used data from all Department of Defense hospitals for the period 1 August 1991 to 31 July 1999 to estimate rates of hospitalisation from any cause. This analysis did not support the hypothesis that Gulf War veterans have an increased risk of post-war morbidity from exposure to Kuwaiti oil well smoke. Although there have been no such UK studies, there is no reason to believe that UK Gulf War veterans would have been affected differently. Bale and Lee (2005) found that of Gulf service related organic disease, of which there was little, respiratory diseases were most common. Asthma was the most common, but no specific triggering agent could be identified.

## Insecticides/Pesticides/Organophosphates

The use of organophosphates (Ops) in the Gulf War was first raised in the UK in May 1996, as a result of which the Organophosphate Pesticide Investigation Team (OPPIT) was set up. Much has been made of exposure to these agents as a result of troops living in tentage in desert situations. However, most tent spraying (swing fogging) was undertaken by trained environmental health officers and not one case of a veteran of any nationality developing acute OP poisoning was described during Op Granby. The situation of veterans during the Gulf conflict should not be confused with the perennial fairly high dose exposure to sheep dip of farmers in the UK/USA/Australia (RCP, 1998). Many UK veterans had been previously exposed to these agents, often for longer periods, whilst on exercises in Belize or Kenya without adverse effects. The substantive report by OPPIT was presented to the House of Commons in December 1996, and stated that Ops had been used but that no evidence of ill-health effects had been found.

There is little convincing evidence in scientific/medical literature to support the theory that low level exposures to nerve agents such as sarin, cyclosarin or tabun (organophosphate warfare nerve agents) can result in long-term health problems (Gerr, 1998). This is unlike the situation of a single high-dose exposure with immediate clinical effects or repeated long-term low dose exposures that may be followed by a delayed peripheral neuropathy (Clegg and Van Gemert, 1999).

The whole scenario is succinctly put by Riddle *et al.* (2003), who wrote, 'In the absence of exposure sufficient to produce observable acute health effects, there is no medical basis to infer that exposures to chemical warfare agents, if such exposures occurred, were of sufficient magnitude to be responsible for any of the symptoms or health concerns among Gulf War veterans'.

Another potential aspect of organophosphate-induced ill health in Gulf veterans arose from the studies of Haley *et al.* (1999). They associated neurologic symptom complexes in Gulf War veterans to low PON1 type Q (type A) amylesterase activity. However, once again their study was flawed by the low numbers studied, 25 symptomatic Gulf veterans and 20 healthy controls, and furthermore they did not measure PON1 mass or diazoxon hydrolysis. Did their work really indicate differences in individual susceptibility? Was it a question of chicken and egg – which came first, symptoms or depletion of PON1 type activity?

Mackness *et al.* (2000) subsequently reported on a study to determine PON1 concentrations in 152 Gulf veterans claiming 'Gulf War syndrome' self-reporting via questionnaire, and 152 age and gender matched controls. They found that in Gulf War veterans, paraoxanase hydrolysis was less than 50 % of that found in controls, but this effect was independent of the effect of PON1 genotype. They noted no difference in the rate of diazoxon hydrolysis between the two groups. They concluded that a decreased capacity to detoxify OP pesticides resulting from low serum PON1 activity may have contributed to the development of 'Gulf War syndrome'. If this were really the case, why were there not more immediately reported cases of alleged OP exposures and health consequences during deployment?

These studies were followed up by Hotopf et al. (2003) in order to determine whether or not PON1 activity was decreased among symptomatic Gulf veterans compared to asymptomatic Gulf veterans, and if Gulf veterans as a whole had lower PON1 activity compared to other military groups (Era and Bosnia). This study unfortunately lacked healthy veterans for the Era and Bosnia groups. They found the two Gulf groups had similar PON1 activity, but personnel deployed to the Gulf had lower PON1 activity compared with those who did not go to the Gulf. They could only speculate about the differences seen. Hotopf et al. suggested that maybe Gulf veterans were exposed to a specific hazard that led to long-term decrease in PON1 activity. Candidate exposures were pyridostigmine bromide, organophosphate pesticides, DEET (a non-OP insect repellent), and even multiple vaccines, but no strong correlations were found. Importantly, although PON1 activity was reduced in Gulf veterans compared with other military groups, the effect is independent of ill health found in Gulf veterans. Hence Haley et al.'s original speculations have not been replicated.


## Psychological Stressors

Not surprisingly, there is now an abundance of international research to show that all veterans, whether symptomatic or not, experience stress as a result of combat. Yet a soldier does not necessarily need to be in the front line of action to experience such stress. Being away from one's family, being inexperienced, not knowing what the physical threat might be, these all constitute stressors as well as being in front line action, firing guns, hand-to-hand fighting, aircraft attacks, and other real or imagined events (Binder and Campbell, 2004). These authors, interestingly, underline how individuals are often poor historians, are likely to omit history of severe stressors or psychiatric problems and, as a result, increase their risk of suffering from physiological forms of stress.

There are many similarities in the constellation of symptoms following large conflicts, and although the labels given to these change with time, e.g. from disordered action of the heart (Da Costa syndrome), neurasthenia, shell shock, combat stress, Gulf War Syndrome, the basic symptoms remain the same, with only a shift on emphasis (Hyams *et al.*, 1996). Which bodily system bears the brunt of attention depends upon public, medical and cultural perceptions at the time (Jones and Wessely, 2005). That there is a real psychological cost to war is undisputed (Friedman, 1996). Psychological stressors do cause significant health problems amongst veterans, but often because of their inability to discuss such problems, or lack of knowledge of specific problems by the attending doctor/counsellor, their psychiatric diagnosis may be missed until long after the conflict.

Furthermore, in some quarters, particularly veterans' activist groups, there has been a reluctance to accept psychological stressors as the cause of ill health, thereby delaying readily available treatment for afflicted veterans. Military attitudes are changing and recognising the psychological cost of warfare. However, how these present depends very much upon prevailing cultural attitudes.

Equally it is understood that it is not possible to screen out Service personnel who may react adversely to stress at the front line or in the theatre of conflict. There is no doubt that post-traumatic stress disorder (PTSD) is an unavoidable consequence of war, a point increasingly recognised since Vietnam, the Falklands and Gulf War I. This in turn results from better understanding of the psychiatric condition and, of course, as a result of much better Internet and website communication. Treatment strategies are now available for sufferers of PTSD, not to mention other psychiatric disorders, and hence veterans become more willing to avail themselves of same without feeling that they bear any social/military stigmata.

A wide-ranging review of chemical warfare and the Gulf War and the impact on Gulf veterans' health (Riddle *et al.*, 2003) concluded that it was most unlikely that Gulf veterans are suffering the chronic effects from illnesses caused by chemical warfare nerve agent exposure, echoing the views of Spencer *et al.* (2001). In this review, Riddle recorded that extensive investigation and review by several expert panels had determined that no evidence exists that chemical warfare nerve agents were used during the Gulf War. Interestingly, he commented that at no time before, during or after the war, was there any confirmation of symptoms among anyone, military or civilian, caused by chemical warfare agent exposure. Nevertheless, he noted that in studies of Gulf War veterans, where a belief existed that chemical weapons were used, this was significantly associated with both severe and mild-to-moderate illnesses. Similarly, those UK veterans with a belief that they have 'Gulf War syndrome' are likely to know someone else with similar beliefs, to have a large number of symptoms, and to have a poor sociological background (Chalder *et al.*, 2001). A number of studies have shown that the psychological impact of a chemical warfare attack, either actual or perceived, can result in immediate and long-term health consequences. Riddle noted, as have others, and we have found at GVMAP, that deployment or war related health impact from life-threatening experiences of the Gulf War, including perceived exposure to chemical warfare agents, should be considered as an important cause of morbidity amongst Gulf War veterans.

## Media

In their quest for an immediate story, the media have much to answer for and could be described as an 'infective vector' in disseminating ill health amongst veterans as a result of irresponsible coverage (Gabriel *et al.*, 2002). The media have promulgated such ideas as vaccinations causing 'Gulf War syndrome' or autoimmune disease resulting in osteoporosis; depleted uranium causing brain damage; organophosphates causing peripheral and central nervous system damage, and NAPS (PB), in isolation or in combination with other factors, also causing an array of diseases.

The effect of media reporting and over-emphasising Gulf veteran health issues is clearly shown in the Combined Analysis of the VA and DoD Gulf War Clinical Evaluation Programmes (2002). There were repeated peaks in referral rates after various releases concerning such issues as the Khamisayah arms dump demolitions, various neurological research preliminary reports, and articles about birth defects. Likewise, at GVMAP there were surges in referral rates after media reports concerning organophosphates 1995/6, vaccinations 1997/8 and DU 1999/2000. Referrals of increased birth defects amongst offspring of Gulf War veterans also occurred as a result of media speculation, media claims of transmission of ill health from a Gulf veteran to other members of the family, and claims of increased mortality amongst Gulf War veterans.

However, fortunately, 14 years on, none of these media speculations has proved correct. Indeed, it is a finding of clinicians who investigate Gulf War health issues, that veterans often come for an assessment because they are distressed by what they have read in the press and are not sure of its meaning. It is the view of the author that for many veterans irresponsible media coverage has caused more health issues for veterans than actually serving in the Gulf itself. There have been too many anecdotal statements in the press that have been blown out of all proportion by politicians and other activist groups, often resulting in enormous amounts of money being spent on various activities, including research, with no beneficial effect for the veterans themselves (Deahl, 2005a, b; Lee, 2005).

It is highly irresponsible of media networks to have caused so much distress among veterans, particularly by suggestions that birth defects and pregnancy problems are more common amongst the spouses of Gulf veterans. Repeated media publications suggesting an increased mortality rate amongst veterans has never been confirmed in robust studies on both sides of the Atlantic (Kang and Bullman, 1999; MacFarlane *et al.*, 2000: DASA six-monthly reports, 2005; 2006). In fact, the opposite is clear – there is no increased mortality amongst veterans as a result of organic disease. There is no unusual pattern of disease amongst veterans (Bale and Lee, 2005). However, the media, for whatever reason, seem reluctant to publish the outcome of such positive publications. Moreover, certain politicians with vested interests, and partly from ignorance, carry on supporting illogical claims about health concerns as a result of service in the Gulf.

Nevertheless, the media could have a positive, responsible, role to play if there were better health risk communication between medical, media and public bodies, thus modifying health-care-seeking behaviour from panic to a rational approach (Smith *et al.*, 2002b).

Over $250 million and £12 million have been spent researching illnesses in veterans of the 1990–91 Gulf War. In spite of that, the nature and cause of such illnesses and/or multiple symptoms remains controversial. As Hotopf and Wessely (2005) pointed out, there are many reasons for this continuing situation and problems of low response rates to questionnaire-based research, ascertainment bias, recall bias and problems identifying suitable control groups, and problems defining health outcomes, were identified. As is generally accepted, many studies of Gulf veterans health were carried out some years after the conflict, when sensationalist media interest and the use of websites by activist groups had potentially biased much evidence based on recall.

# REFERENCES

Abou-Donia, M. B., Wilmarhk, R., Abdel-Rahman, A. A., Jensen, K. F., Oehme, F. W., and Kurt, T. L. (1996). Neurotoxicity resulting from co-exposure to pyridostigmine bromide, DEET and permethrin; implications for Gulf War chemical exposures, *Journal of Toxicology and Environmental Health*, **48**, 35–56.

Asa, P. B., Cao, Y. and Garry, R. F. (2000). Antibodies to squalene in Gulf War syndrome, *Experimental Molecular Pathology*, **68**, 55–64.

Bale, A. J. and Lee, H. A. (2005) An observational study on diagnoses of 3233 Gulf Veterans (Op Granby 1990–91) who attended the Ministry of Defence's Medical Assessment Programme 1993–2004, *Journal of the Royal Naval Medical Service*, **91**(2), 99–111.

Binder, L. M. and Campbell, K. A. (2004). Medically unexplained symptoms and neuropsychological assessment, *J. Clin. Exper. Neuropsychology*, **26**, 369–92.

Bolton, J. P. G. and Foster, C. R. M. (2002). Battlefield use of depleted uranium and the health of veterans, *Trauma*, **4**, 1–10.

Bolton, J. P. G., Lee, H. A. and Gabriel, R. (2001). Letter: Vaccinations as risk factors for ill health in veterans of the Gulf War, *British Medical Journal*, **322**, 361.

British National Formulary (2004). *Anticholinesterases – Pyridostigmine*, **48**, 514–5.

Chalder, T., Hotopf, M., Unwin, C., Hull, L., Ismail, K., D. A. and Wessely, S. (2001). Prevalence of Gulf War veterans who believe they have Gulf War Syndrome: questionnaire study, *British Medical Journal*, **323**, 473–76.

Chaney, L. A., Wineman, R. W., Rockhold, R. W. and Hume, A. S. (2000). Acute effects of an insect repellent N, N-diethyl-m-toluamide (DEET) on cholinesterase inhibition induced by pyridostigmine bromide (PB) in rats, *Toxicol. Appl. Pharmacol.*, **165**, 170–114.

Clegg, D. J. and Van Gemert, M. (1999). Expert panel report of human studies of chlorpyrifas and/or other organophosphate exposures, *Journal of Toxicology and Environmental Health* B, *Crit. Rev.*, **2**, 257–79.

DoD and VA Gulf War Clinical Evaluation Programs (2002). A study of the clinical findings from systematic medical examinations of 100 339 US Gulf War veterans, Veterans Health Administration and Department of Defense, Washington, DC.

Deahl, M. P. (2005a). Smoke, mirrors and Gulf War illness, *Lancet*, **365**, 635–8.

Deahl, M. P. (2005b). Gulf War illness, *British Journal of Hospital Medicine*, **66**(10), 608.

Defence Analytical Services Agency (DASA). (2006). http:/www.dsa.mod.uk/natstats/gulf/intro.html

Donta, S. T., Engel, C. C., Collins, J. F. *et al.* (2004). Benefits and harms of Doxycycline treatment for Gulf War Veterans' illnesses. A randomized, double-blind, placebo-controlled trial, *Annals of Internal Medicine*, **141**(2), 85–93.

Enstone, J. E., Wale, M. C. J., Nguyen-van-Tam, J. S. and Pearson, J. C. G. (2003). Adverse medical events in British service personnel following anthrax vaccination. *Vaccine*, **21**, 1348–54.

Friedman, M. J. (2004). Acknowledging the psychiatric cost of war, *New England Journal of Medicine*, **351**, 75–7.

Friedman, A., Kaufer, D., Shemer, J., Hendler, I., Soreq, H. and Tur-Kaspai, N. (1996). Pyridostigmine brain penetration under stress enhances neuronal excitability and induces early transcriptal response, *Native Medicine*, **2**, 1382–5.

Gabriel, R., Bolton, J. P. G., Bale, A. J. and Lee, H. A. (2002). Letter: Gulf War syndrome may be post-conflict dysfunction, *British Medical Journal*, **324**, 914.

Gerr, F. (1998). *Health Effects of Neurotoxic Agents in the Persian Gulf War*. A report to the Committee on Veterans' Affairs of the United States Senate, Washington DC: US Senate.

Grauer, E., Alkalai, D., Kapon, J., Cohen, G., Rave, A., *et al.* (2000). Stress does not enable pyridostigmine bromide to inhibit brain cholinesterase after parenteral administration, *Toxicol. Applied Pharmacol.*, **164**, 301–4.

Gray, G. C., Reed, R. J., Kaiser, K. S., Smith, T. C. and Gastaniaga, V. M. (2002). Self-reported symptoms and medical conditions amongst 11 868 Gulf War-era veterans – the Seabee health study, *American Journal of Epidemiology*, **155**, 1033–43.

Greenberg, N., Wessely, S., Iversen, A., Hull, L., Unwin, C. and Destrange, M. (2003). Vaccination records in Gulf War veterans, *Journal of Occupational and Environmental Medicine*, **45**, 219–21.

Greenberg, N., Iversen, A. C., Unwin, C., Hull, L. and Wessely, S. (2004). Screening for depleted uranium in the United Kingdom armed forces: who wants it and why, *J. Epidemiol. Comm. Health*, **58**, 558–61.

Griffiths, G. D., Hornby, R. J., Stevens, D. J., Scott, L. A. M. and Upshall, D. G. ( 2001). Biological consequences of multiple vaccine and pyridostigmine pre-treatment in the guinea pig, *Journal of Applied Toxicology*, **21**, 59–68.

Haley, R. W. and Kurt, T. (1997). Self-reported exposure to neurotoxic chemical combinations in the Gulf War: a cross-sectional epidemiologic study *Journal of the American Medical Association*, **277**, 231–37.

Haley, R. W., Kurt, T. and Hom, J. (1997). Is there a Gulf War Syndrome? Searching for syndromes by factor analysis of symptoms, *Journal of the American Medical Association*, **277**, 215–22.

Haley, R. and Billecke, S., la Du, B. (1999). Association of low PON1 Type Q (type A) amylesterase activity with neurologic symptom complexes in Gulf War veterans, *Journal of Toxicology and Applied Pharmacology*, **157**, 227–33.

Health Protection Agency (Centre for Infections) (2005). webteam@hpa.org.uk.

Heller, J. M. (1992). *Kuwait Oil Fire Health Risk Assessment*, Washington, DC: US Army Center for Health Promotion and Preventive Medicine.

Hotopf, M. and Wessely, S. (2005). Can epidemiology clear the fog of war? Lessons from the 1990-91 Gulf War, *International Journal of Epidemiology*, 1021.

Hotopf, M., Hull, L., Ismail, K., *et al.* (2000). The role of vaccinations as risk factors for ill-health in veterans of the Persian Gulf War, *British Medical Journal*, **320**, 1363–67.

Hotopf, M., Mackness, M. I., Nikolaou, V., Collier, D. A., Curtis, C., David, A., Durrington, P., Hull, L., Ismail, K., Peaklan, M., Unwin, C., Wessely, S. and Mackness, B. (2003). Paraoxanase in Persian Gulf War Veterans, *Journal of Occupational and Environmental Medicine*, **45**, 668–75.

Hyams, K. C., Hanson, K., Wignall, F. S., Escamilla, J. and Oldfield, E. C. (1995). The impact of infectious diseases on the health of US troops deployed to the Persian Gulf during operations Desert Shield and Desert Storm, *Clinical Infectious Diseases*, **20**, 1497–1504.

Hyams, K. C., Wignall, F. S. and Roswell, R. (1996). War syndromes and their evaluation: from the US Civil War to the Persian Gulf War, *Annals of Internal Medicine*, **125**, 398–405.

Ismail, K., Everitt, B., Blatchley, N., Hull, L., Unwin, C., David, A. and Wessely, S. (1999). Is there a Gulf War Syndrome? *Lancet*, **353**, 179–82.

Jones, E. and Wessely, S. (2005). War syndromes: the impact of culture on medically unexplained symptoms, *Medical History*, **49**, 55–78.

Joseph, S. C. (1997). A comprehensive clinical evaluation of 20 000 Persian Gulf War veterans, *Military Medicine*, **162**, 149–55.

Kang, K. and Bullman, T. A. (1999). Mortality among US veterans of the Gulf War: update through December 1997. *Conference on Federally Sponsored Gulf War Veterans' Illnesses Research*, Arlington, Washington, DC, June 23–25, p. 28.

Kant, G. J., Bauman, R. A., Feaster, S. R., Anderson, S. M., Saviolakis, G. A. and Garcia, G. E. (2001). The combined effects of pyridostigmine and chronic stress on brain cortical and blood acetyl cholinesterase, corticosterone, prolactin and alternation performance in rats. *Pharm Biochem Behaviour*, **70**, 209–18.

Laforce, L. M. and Diniega, A. (2000). Recommendations regarding review of the paper 'Antibodies to Squalene in Gulf War Syndrome' by P. B. Asa, Y. Cao and R. F. Garry. DoD (Health Affairs) Armed Forces Epidemiological Board (AFEB), July 2000, Washington DC.

Lallement, G., Fouquin, A., Baubuchon, D., Burckhart, M. F., Carpentier, D. and Canini, F. (1998). Even extreme Stress does not induce penetration of pyridostigmine bromide into the brain of guinea pigs, *Neurotoxicology*, **19**, 759–66.

Lee, H. A. (2005). Comment on 'Gulf War Illness', *British Journal of Hospital Medicine*, **66**(10), 706.

Lee, H. A., Bolton, J. P. G. and Gabriel, R. (2001). Is depleted uranium really a health issue? *Lancet Oncology*, **2**(4):197.

Lee, H. A., Gabriel, R., Bolton, J. P. G., Bale, A. J. and Jackson, M. (2002). Health status and clinical diagnoses in 3000 UK Gulf War veterans, *Journal of the Royal Society of Medicine*, **95**, 491–97.

Lee, H. A., Bale, A. J. and Gabriel, R. (2005). Results of investigations on Gulf War veterans, *Clinical Medicine*, **5**(2), 166–72.

Lo, S.-C., Levin, L., Ribas, J., Chung, R., Wang, R. Y.-H., Wear, D. and Shih, J. W.-K. (2000). Lack of serological evidence for *Mycoplasma fermentans* infection in army Gulf War veterans: a large scale case-control study, *Epidemiol. Infect.*, **125**, 609–16.

Macfarlane, G. J., Thomas, E. and Cherry, N. (2000). Mortality among UK Gulf War veterans, *Lancet*, **356**, 17–21.

Mackness, B., Durrington, P. and Mackness, M. (2000). Low paraoxanase in Persian Gulf War veterans self-reporting Gulf War Syndrome, *Biochem. Biophys. Res. Commun.*, **276**, 725–33.

Magill, A. J., Grogl, M., Gasser, R. A., Sun, W. and Oster, C. N. (1993). Visceral infection caused by *Leishmania tropica* in veterans of Operation Desert Storm, *New England Journal of Medicine*, **328**, 1383–87.

McCauley, L. A., Joos, S. K., Lasarev, M. R., Storzbach, D. and Bourdette, D. N. (1999a). Gulf War unexplained illnesses: persistence and unexplained nature of self-reported symptoms, *Environmental Research*, **81**, 215–23.

McCauley, L., Joos, S., Spencer, P. *et al.* (1999b). Strategies to assess validity of self-reported exposures during the Persian Gulf War, *Environmental Research*, **81**, 195–205.

McDiarmid, M. A. (2001). Depleted uranium and public health – 50 years study of occupational exposure provides little evidence of cancer, *British Medical Journal*, **322**, 123–24.

McDiarmid, M. A., Keogh, J. P., Hooper, F. J., McPhaul, K., Squibb, K., Kane, R., DiPino, R., Kabat, M., Kaup, B., Anderson, L., Hoover, D., Brown, L., Hamilton, M., Jacobson-Kram, D., Burrows, B. and Walsh, M. (2000). Health effects of depleted uranium on exposed Gulf War veterans, *Environmental Research A*, **82**, 168–80.

McDiarmid, M. A., Squibb, K. and Engelhard, S. M. (2004). Biological monitoring for urinary uranium in Gulf War I veterans, *Health Physics*, **87**, 51–6.

McManus, H. (1997). Vaccine clue found to Gulf War Syndrome, *Sunday Times*, 22 June.

MoD (2002). Biological Monitoring Programme (Institute of Naval Medicine) (Administered by DSTL Radiological Protection Service), implements policy introduced in January 2002.

MoD (2005). Review of modeling of the demolitions at Khamisayah in March 1991 and implications for UK personnel, www.mod.uk/issues/gulfwar

Murphy, F. (1999). Gulf War Syndrome. There may be no specific syndrome but troops suffer after most wars, *British Medical Journal*, **318**, 274–75.

Murray, V. S. G., Bailey, M. R. and Spratt, B. G. (2002). Depleted uranium: a new battlefield hazard, *Lancet*, Supplement, **360**, 31–2.

Nicholson, G. L. (1996). Further information on Persian Gulf War illnesses, *Int. J. Occup. Med. Immun. Tox.*, **5**, 83–6.

Nicholson, G. L. and Nicholson, N. L. (1996). Diagnosis and treatment of mycoplasmal infections in Persian Gulf illnesses – CFIDS patient, *Int. J. Occup. Med. Immunol. Tox.*, **5**, 69–78.

Riddle, J. R., Brown, M., Smith, T., Ritchie, E. C., Brix, K. A. and Romano, J. (2003). Chemical warfare and the Gulf War: a Review of the impact on Gulf Veterans' health, *Military Medicine*, **168**, 606–13.

Rijpkema, S. G., Adams, T., Rigsby, P., Xing, D. K. and Corbel, M. J. (2005). Investigation in a model system of the effects of combinations of anthrax and pertussis vaccines administered to Service personnel in the 1991 Gulf War, *Human Vaccines*, **1**(4), 19–23.

Rook, G. A. W. and Zumla, A. (1997). Gulf War Syndrome: is it due to a systemic shift in cytokine balance towards a Th2 profile? *Lancet*, **349**, 1831–33.

Royal College of Physicians and Royal College of Psychiatrists (1998). Organophosphate Sheep Dip: Clinical Aspects of Long Term Low Dose Exposure. Report of a Joint Working Party. London: Royal College of Physicians.

Sen, A. (2002). Health: perception versus observation. Self-reported morbidity has severe limitations and can be extremely misleading, *British Medical Journal*, **324**, 860–61.

Shaheen, S. (2000). Shots in the desert and Gulf War Syndrome – evidence that multiple vaccinations during deployment are to blame is inconclusive, *British Medical Journal*, **320**, 1351–52.

Smith, T. C., *et al.* (2003). Gulf War veterans and Iraqi nerve agents at Khamisayah: post war hospitalization data revisited, *American Journal of Epidemiology*, **158**, 457–67.

Smith, T. C., *et al.* (2004). The post war hospitalization experience of Gulf War veterans pariticipating in US Health Registries, *J. Occup. Environ. Med.*, **46**, 386–97.

Smith, T. C., Heller, J. M., Hooper, T. I., Gackstetter, G. D. and Gray, G. C. (2002a). Are Gulf War veterans experiencing illness due to exposure to smoke from Kuwaiti oil wellfires? Examination of Department of Defense Hospitalization Data, *American Journal of Epidemiology*, **155**, 907–17.

Smith, T. C., Smith, B., Ryan, M. A. K., Gray, G. C., Hooper, T. I., Heller, J. M., Dalager, N. A., Kang, H. K. and Gackstetter, G. D. (2002b). Ten years and 100 000 participants later: occupational and other factors influencing participation in US Gulf War Health Registries, *J. Occup. Environ. Med.*, **44**, 758–69.

Spencer, P. S., Macauley, L. A., Lapidus, J. A., Lazarev, M., Joos, S. K. and Storzbach, D. (2001). Self-reported exposures and their association with unexplained illness in a population based case controlled study of Gulf War veterans, *J. Occup. Environ. Med.*, **42**, 1041–56.

Stevens, D., Scott, E. A. M., Gwyther, R. J., Griffiths, G. D. and Pearce, P. C. (2006). Multiple vaccine and pyridostigmine interactions: effects on cognitive behaviour and muscle function in common marmosets, *Pharmacology, Biochemisty and Behaviour* (in press).

Stewart-Brown, S. and Farmer, A. (1997). Screening could seriously damage your health. Decisions to screen must take account of the social and psychological costs, *British Medical Journal*, **314**, 533.

Unwin, C., Blatchley, N., Coker, W. J., Ferry, S., Hotopf, M., Hull, L., *et al.* (1999). The health of United Kingdom Servicemen who served in the Persian Gulf War, *Lancet*, **353**, 169–78.

Upshall, D. G. (2000). Gulf related illness – current perspectives, *Journal of the Royal Army Medical Corps*, **146**, 13–17.

US Army Environmental Hygiene Agency (1991). Final Report: Kuwait oil fire health risk assessment, No 39, 26-L192-91, 5 May–3 Dec. Aberdeen Proving Ground, Maryland: Department of the Army.

Williams, K. E., Mann, T. M., Chamberlain, S., Wilson, S., Gwyther, R. J., Griffiths, G. D., Scott, E. A. M. and Pearce, P. C. (2006). Multiple vaccine and pyridostigmine interactions: effects on EEG and sleep in common marmosets, *Pharmacology, Biochemistry and Behaviour* (in press).

Winkenwerder, W., *et al.* (2002). Modelling and Risk Characterization af US Demolition Operational at the Khamisayah Pit. Washington DC: Department of Defense.

# 4

# Is GWS About More than the Gulf War? An Anthropological Approach to the Illness

Susie Kilshaw

## INTRODUCTION

This chapter focuses on an anthropological interpretation of GWS and, thus, looks at the illness as a socio-cultural phenomenon. The author argues that when faced with soldiers complaining of a variety of symptoms and illnesses, the medical community should pay heed to the person and the wider context of their lives, for it is revealed in these pages that GWS was more extensive than the Gulf War. One must ask what else is happening in the lives of these people besides their malaise. Furthermore, the author argues that it is important to understand sufferer's perceptions and understandings of their disorder so that consensus can be reached. Relevant themes that emerge from veterans' explanatory models of their illness are discussed; issues such as a focus on conspiracy theories and the stigma of mental illness. Importantly, the question is raised as to whether or not the process of medicalisation is an appropriate way to frame the problem.

Based on 14 months' ethnographic fieldwork in the UK, the data for this research project was collected between September 2001 and November 2002 from in-depth interviews, participant observation and

*War and Health: Lessons from the Gulf War*   Edited by Harry Lee & Edgar Jones
© 2007 John Wiley & Sons, Ltd

document analysis. The primary data are in-depth interviews with core activists, Gulf War veterans, doctors, scientists, and others involved in the GWS movement. A total of 93 interviews were conducted, 67 of which were with UK veterans. The main informants for this project represent a particular group of active GWS sufferers who, although not necessarily representative of Gulf veterans as a whole, have been influential in lobbying for media support and representation. These veterans have driven the GWS movement and, in many ways, represent the public face of Gulf War Syndrome sufferers. Importantly, this group of veterans have influenced lay perceptions of the illness and, thus, they may not be a representative group, but they are an important group.

It has been shown that from a medical point of view (Gray and Kang, 2006; Ismail and Lewis, 2006) that GWS is a misnomer, since no new illness or symptom cluster unique to Gulf War veterans has been identified. Having said that, it is likely that 'GWS' will continue to be used to describe the medical legacy of the war. As an anthropologist, the author focuses on the experiences and understandings of those who believe they are suffering from GWS and, thus, refers to the illness as they do. The veterans spoken about in this chapter referred to their illness as 'Gulf War Syndrome', and they believed it to be a unique, discrete, organic pathology caused by toxic exposures in the Gulf. It is a syndrome in that this is the way they understand, perceive and experience it. The meaning 'of a disease category cannot be understood simply as a set of defining symptoms. It is rather a "syndrome" of typical experiences, a set of words, experiences, and feelings which typically "run together" for the members of a society' (Good, 1977, p. 27).

Such a 'syndrome is not merely a reflection of symptoms linked with each other in natural reality, but a set of experiences associated through networks of meaning and social interaction in society. This conception of medical semantics directs our attention to the use of medical discourse to articulate the experience of distinctive patterns of social stress, to the use of illness language to negotiate relief for the sufferer, and thus to the constitution of the meaning of medical language in its use in a variety of communicative contexts' (Good, 1977, p. 27). It is these webs of associations that give meaning and depth to experience and through understanding these connections present in GWS discourse that is looked at here.

Anthropology has revealed that there is a relationship between how social and physical bodies are perceived. The 'social body constrains the way the physical body is perceived. The physical experience of the body, always modified by the social categories through which it is known, sustains a particular view of society' (Douglas, 1970, p. 65). The body, then, constitutes a 'natural symbol' (the representational uses of the body as a natural symbol with which to think about nature, society and culture). The body in health is a model of organic wholeness, whilst the body in sickness offers a model of social disease, conflict, and disintegration; reciprocally, society in sickness or health offers a model for understanding the body. To understand GWS and how it is experienced by sufferers more fully, the scope of analysis must be broadened. GWS is about much more than the Gulf War, so an analysis of the problem must look at the individual in their cultural and social context. Furthermore, whereas medical analysis will focus on the individual body, on symptoms as biomedical entities, and the individual's war exposures/ experiences, this author calls for a widening of the frame to include other relevant aspects of a person's life. An account of the individual's local social worlds (Kleinman and Kleinman, 1991) – those shared interpersonal experiences that take place in the immediate domains of family, community and workplace – is essential to an adequate understanding of the condition. Features such as Euro-American culture (including health beliefs and anxieties), military culture, military experience, and post-war experience, are all considered in this more holistic investigation.

Good (1977) suggests that the medical model of disease holds 'certain basic and often unrecognised assumptions about the relationship of language to medicine and about the nature of the way in which meaning of medical language is constituted' (p.27). Furthermore, he argues that such assumptions present obstacles to our understanding of the role of psychosocial and cultural factors in disease. Illness is an innately cultural experience, for illness is our personal expression and response to disease and/or suffering. Disease refers to 'abnormalities in the structure and/or function of organs, pathological states whether or not they are culturally recognized.' Illness, however, 'refers to a person's perceptions and experiences of socially disvalued states including, but not limited to, disease' (Young, 1982, p. 264). We do not experience illness at the level of viruses or cells, indeed, we can 'experience anything at all only through and by means of culturally constructed socially reproduced structures of metaphor and meaning' (DiGiacomo, 1992, p. 117). As we can only experience and understand illness through these culturally constructed structures, it is pertinent that we investigate them to understand fully a condition such as GWS. The 'meaning of illness term is not constituted simply by its relationship to a "disease", whether defined as a set of characteristic symptoms or as a physiological state. The meaning of an illness term is rather constituted by its linking together in a potent image a complex of symbols, feelings, and stresses, thus being deeply integrated into the structure of a community and its culture' (Good, 1977, p. 48). And the meaning of an illness term is constituted as it is used in social interaction to articulate the experience of distress, and to bring about action that will relieve that distress.

Illness narratives convey meaning to the individual and those around them, but there are also narratives of the body through symptoms and body signs. GWS can be seen as a system of thought and an idiom of distress. By looking at the narratives of sufferers and those around them, we see that GWS is both a unique expression and way of making sense of the life-worlds of a particular group of people as well as being a product of wider social issues. GWS is wider than the Gulf War; it is characteristic of the anxieties and beliefs of late-Twentieth century life. There are other things happening in the lives of these men (and women) that they are trying to explain and the package is unique. One can examine the way in which illnesses are formed by fitting into the existing illness models and the way in which bodily vulnerability is supported by wider social beliefs. GWS emerged and gained media attention because it both responded to and conformed to existing illness beliefs and anxieties. Simultaneously, it was formed by these pre-existing cultural beliefs. GWS has been constructed, framed and articulated by particular themes that are relevant to society such as: anxiety about health, erosion of faith in science and doctors, the centrality of the immune system to their beliefs, and notions of risk.

## SYMPTOMS AND SYMPTOM REPORTING AS IDIOMS OF DISTRESS

Symptoms are used to talk about and negotiate matters other than bodily illness (Kirmayer, 1996). Somatic symptoms are the most common individual expression of social problems and emotional distress (Kirmayer and Young, 1988) and are referred to as 'idioms of distress' (Nichter, 1981; Kirmayer, 1996). Symptoms are 'not disarticulated entities that have a phenomenological reality independent of culture, even though it is the culture of contemporary science' (Obeyesekere, 1985, p. 150). Symptoms are fused into a conception. Thus, when one is confronted with an individual who is presenting a series of symptoms, one must be aware that this process is more complicated than just an individual communicating a direct physical experience or reality. In an anthropological inquiry, illness symptoms are not only 'biological entities', but can also be conceptualised as 'coded metaphors that speak to the contradictory aspects of social life, expressing feelings, sentiments, and ideas that must otherwise be kept hidden' (Scheper, Hughes and Lock, 1986, p. 138–39). That is to say, physical symptoms can be seen as part of a process of making meaning out of experience. Furthermore, there is a collective aspect of symptom and symptom language.

The work of other anthropologists on medically unexplained syndromes has shed light on how social forms of distress can be played out on individual bodies. The 'symptoms of CFS may represent the embodied experience and expression of social sources of distress' (Ware, 1993, p. 68). Referring to the 1983–7 Australian epidemic of repetitive strain injury (RSI), Kirmayer suggests that RSI 'became an emblem of other social problems in Australia: work dissatisfaction, the socio-economic plight of migrants, and concerns about the impact of automation in the workplace, as well as idiosyncratic issues of individuals' (Kirmayer, 1999, p. 277). RSI functioned rhetorically as 'a polysemic metaphor not only for what ailed the Australian workforce, for what ails Australian society' (Reid and Reynold, 1990, p. 185). Similarly, it is important to view the way in which GWS can be seen as a metaphor of experience and how it may not be helpful for it to be medicalised, as such a process allows the social and political origins of such suffering to be overlooked.

Others scholars have argued that GWS is a cultural phenomenon (e.g. Showalter, 1997) and the author's interpretation of GWS has been influenced by such work, but goes further by investigating the specifics of GWS. Such a reading looks at GWS as a particular cultural phenomenon, not just one expression of a wider social trend. Showalter (1997) sees GWS as an expression of modern-day hysteria and suggests that it is simply one manifestation of a larger cultural phenomenon. It is a cultural symptom of anxiety and stress and, thus, she sees GWS and its related illnesses as entirely psychological: it is the manifestation and expression of the psyche. A literary critic and historian of medicine, Showalter's theory therefore lacks a historical or anthropological reading of these disorders. By lumping them all together as manifestations of the same thing, she ignores the way that each of these conditions is unique and responds to different issues. An anthropological account goes beyond such a reading and asks how did we get to this state of affairs, from where did it develop and what is happening in culture and society that helps to form such a situation. Showalter's analysis ignores the differences between these very diverse illnesses and by so doing lacks a real understanding of the conditions themselves and the unique factors that give rise to them.

Any serious analysis of illnesses such as GWS should 'probably begin by reversing this rhetorical move and turning 'somatisation' back into its 'raw observable, medically unexplained symptoms' (Kirmayer, 1999, p. 272). When reduced simply to symptoms of a disorder, the meaningful and social dimension of distress may be lost (Kirmayer, 1999). There is a need, then to understand sufferers' accounts, the symptoms themselves and the context within which we find them in order to better understand what was being expressed and commented upon. GWS is characteristic of the society in which it is found. It emerged out of common health anxieties and beliefs and was simultaneously moulded by them. The media seized hold of and fuelled this story because it made sense: a story about soldiers made ill, their immune systems ravaged, by an onslaught of toxins and chemicals at the hand of their own government simply rang true.

## THE NARRATIVE CONSTRUCTION OF GWS

It is 'very often when narratives are most personal that they draw upon the deep structures of the cultures to which they belong' (Skultans, 2000, p. 11). Narrative is a 'fundamental human way of giving meaning to experience' and through telling and interpreting experiences, narrative mediates between the inner world and the outer world (Garro and Mattingly, 2000, p. 1). In medical anthropology, narrative has come to be seen as the way individuals make sense of chaotic life events such as trauma and illness. In previous work, the author has illustrated the way in which veterans learn a culturally specific narrative (Kilshaw, 2004). Forming an identity around GWS enables a veteran to make sense of all their experiences: it provides coherence. As an extremely robust and flexible system of thought, GWS narratives focus on the way in which the war provides a filter through which all of their negative post-war experiences can be understood and given meaning. A rash, marriage difficulties, and vulnerability to colds, can all be linked together in one sweeping system. The GWS narrative provides a meta narrative: a 'grand theory,' a narrative about narratives. A meta narrative is a story we tell about ourselves, what we do, and what is expected; it is a story that links our smaller stories together and gives us unity (social, psychological, and intellectual). It is an overarching story which provides the frame of reference for all other stories. One cannot deny the magnetism of such a comprehensive and elegant system of explanation. Such diagnoses and their accompanying movements, give the sufferer the sense that everything is connected and explainable and that someone else is to blame.

In the face of uncertainty and a lack of satisfactory answers to explain their suffering, veterans searched for an explanation that resonated with their experience. In the GWS narrative they were able to reconstruct their identity. Importantly, such a label provides connections with positive aspects of their former soldier identity. It is important to note the web of meanings and associations that would accompany labelling oneself a GWS sufferer. Saying one is a GWS sufferer highlights the fact that the individual had been a soldier, had been to war, had been employed. If we follow these associations further we can see that these roles would be linked to notions of the sufferer being once strong, fit, healthy, masculine and potent. A diagnosis of GWS reminds the sufferer and those around him, that he fought, that he was once a strong, masculine man who made the utmost sacrifice for his country: he went to war. Through the GWS narrative their identity remains linked to their previous role as a solider; this connection is strengthened and brought to the forefront.

Narratives are produced in dialogue with those around them, but the shared construction of a narrative also connects people and strengthens the mutual aspects of the narrative. Stacey's cultural study of cancer suggests that for many cancer patients, 'relating their stories is integral to their recovery,' but patients' narratives also bind people together as they emphasise similarity between patients. In this sense, 'narrative might be seen more positively as an important mechanism for recognition and, for many, for sanity' (Stacey, 1997, p. 16). Through interacting with other sufferers the interpretations of the group become those of the individual. Furthermore, movement participants 'learn to construct meaning in particular ways through the frames supported by the movement' (Shriver *et al.*, 2002, p. 125). The collective narrative orders and provides meaning for the individual's illness experience of chaos and unravelling. Simultaneously, the individual's narrative contributes support for the collective narrative. As GWS sufferers 'interact and adopt new cultural codes, they are further integrated into a movement, and the solidarity of the group is strengthened' (Shriver *et al.*, 2002, p. 125). The GWS narrative provides veterans with a way to reconstruct their identity and offers a meaningful explanation for their experience of disruption.

The veterans' associations played a key role in developing that connection with their former warrior. Associations are created along military lines and mirror aspects of military life. Furthermore, ascribing to an identity as a GWS sufferer meant membership to a community of other sufferers and, importantly, to other soldiers. By and large the veterans interviewed for this work had left the military soon after the Gulf War: within months or a few years of the Gulf War they were made redundant; lost their military identity which they valued so highly. Many described the transition from military to civilian life as extremely difficult: they simply could not fit into civilian culture or find suitable work. The GWS community embraces the sufferer and provides support and comradeship, something which many explained they had sorely missed when they left the military. When discussing the association, many veterans describe a feeling of belonging, and suggested it was 'one big family.' They explain that other members were similar to them; they shared an understanding of military life and of the illness. The support groups are structured around military lines. Although bitter towards the forces, the veterans were surprisingly loyal to the military ethos.

It has been suggested that GWS is spread by word of mouth (Showalter, 1997; Chalder *et al.*, 2001). Chalder *et al.* suggest that those with the illness were much more likely to be in contact with others who were ill with GWS. Such findings support the view of the mainstream GWS research community that often hint at veterans' groups as being damaging to veteran's health. The author would suggest that it is not as simple as that, for GWS support groups provided a necessary service in a vacuum. They provided support and a community for a group of struggling veterans facing a period of uncertainty and isolation upon leaving the forces. Support groups played a role in enabling veterans to re-configure their identity and gave them the means to create a continuity of self. For a veteran who left the forces with its accompanying status, community and structure, the move to civilian life was often exceedingly fraught. The GWS support groups provided people with an anchor, a sense of self and a link with their past identity as a soldier, an employed man, a fit man: a man who was valued.

The associations are central in enabling the veteran to re-configure their post-war/post-forces identity in that they provide a template that can accommodate veterans' unique experiences and create a biographical narrative. The support groups and the GWS narrative helped veterans to make sense of their experiences and find meaning in them. It is a very natural process and one that we all experience, for modernity has impacted the self and the way the self is constructed (Beck, 1992; Giddens, 1991). Socially prescribed biography is 'transformed into biography that is self-produced and continues to be produced' (Beck, 1992, p. 135). Dumit (2006) has argued that new illness movements, like GWS, provide such 'construction kits of biographical combinations' (Beck, 1992, p. 135): a kind of identity DIY. He points out that one place where we can directly see this active, reflexive theorizing of society and one's place in it, is on the Internet, where these illness movements have websites and use net discussion groups, such as we see with the Gulf veterans and their associations. Thus, illness movements such as GWS and CFS are, in part, a conscious struggle over the power to construct new identities, to reinterpret norms and to reshape institutions (Melucci, 1989 and 1996b in Dumit, 2006).

Gulf War associations provide an identity for sufferers and an explanatory model for the veterans' experience of disruption. As Dumit (2006, pp. 581–2, 589) suggests:

'New social movements around health represent collective action in the face of the individualizing of problems at every level (Melucci, 1996a). Collective sharing of personal narratives helps show that psychological blame ("It's all in your head") and psychological responses ("Why me?") are structurally produced and can be resisted. New social movements in general provide the space and time for creatively and meaningful construction of new experiences and social roles (Melucci, 1996b). . . . Collective sharing of useful information is another primary purpose of new social movements as described by Melucci. Individuals who are otherwise isolated and having to face institutions on their own, are able to draw upon the collected experiences of others in order to navigate these sites of struggle, including courts, insurance agencies, mass media, and government. Most of these institutions depend upon control over the flow of information and impersonal procedures for their smooth running. The collective wisdom of individual experiences offers powerful modes of resistance to this kind of power.'

Illnesses and the movements that appear around them are entwined with identity. Illness provides a way to make sense of life events and allows one to develop an effective and robust identity. The problem is that this identity and community is wholly built around an illness. Illness remains at the centre of an organization with almost all of the members being ill themselves. It appears that to be a member, one had to be ill and attribute the illness to the Gulf War. What seems to have occurred is that identity as a soldier becomes embedded in identity as a sick, wronged, poisoned soldier. The narrative around GWS is one of being wronged, of being poisoned and of never getting better. Thus, they remain in a liminal position, they are 'betwixt and between', neither one status nor the other and are in a state of ambiguity.

Freud 'made us aware of the persuasive power of the coherent narrative – in particular, the way in which an aptly chosen reconstruction can fill the gap between two apparently unrelated events, and in the process, make sense out of nonsense' (Spence, 1982, p. 21). Contemporary psychotherapeutic practices 'continue to stress the role of narrative in decoding and reframing the past to make sense of the present and provide an orientation for the future' (Garro and Mattingly, 2000, p. 7). Eisenberg (1981) has suggested that an important aspect of medical encounter is the co-construction of a plausible account between patient and healer. The patient has a coherent explanation that leaves him no longer feeling the victim of the inexplicable and uncontrollable, and the amelioration of symptoms often results (Eisenberg, 1981, p. 245, in Garro and Mattingly, 2000). As stories are told they can become simplified, so 'good narratives can be beneficial in making our complex experiences more simple and understandable but, at the same time, they distort our recollection of them' (Pennebaker, 2003, p. 27). It is necessary to be aware of an individual's illness narrative and how it is constructed in association with others. Illness narratives are not static and are constantly evolving and this may be one way to offer assistance to veterans: to find new ways of framing and understanding their illness.

## GWS EXPLANATORY MODELS

Anthropology stresses the importance of focusing on classification and on understanding rationality in social and cultural contexts. For a social fact, such as illness, can only be known and made intelligible through investigating the context in which it emerged. In order fully to understand an illness, particularly one that is surrounded by so much debate, one must grasp what it feels like to have the condition. It is essential that we understand how GWS is lived and experienced by those caught in its throes. People often have very different ways of understanding illness and its consequences, and the best treatment: a different explanatory model. Beliefs and convictions can be collapsed into the notion of an explanatory model and it is necessary to understand an individual's model of their illness and work with it. This approach could offer a helpful starting point for future meetings between the clinical world and the post-combat soldier.

Research has noted the problems with self-reported measures of exposure. Although these accounts may provide inaccurate estimates of Gulf

War exposures, self-reports reveal important information about the individual's beliefs concerning toxic exposures and their beliefs about how these exposures affect their current health problems. Furthermore these beliefs 'will influence veterans' emotional (e.g. patterns of distress) and behavioural (e.g. self-care and health-care use) responses to symptoms' (Hunt *et al.*, 2004, p. 819). People's beliefs and attitudes about illness are particularly important for a number of behavioural health outcomes, such as help seeking, treatment compliance, functional impairment, and course and chronicity of symptoms (Ewart *et al.*, 1986; Sensky, 1997, in Hunt *et al.*, 2004). Understanding a veteran's explanatory model and theory of causation is central, as this will likely impact symptom severity (Chalder *et al.*, 2001; Boyd and Hallman *et al.*, 2004). When 'medical uncertainty is high, as is the case for MUPS (medically unexplained physical symptoms/syndrome), it is reasonable to expect that idiosyncratic illness beliefs may have a larger impact on clinical outcome than might be the case for conditions with scientifically established etiologies' (Hunt *et al.*, 2004, p. 819).

## The Role of Conspiracy Theory

A key aspect of the GWS explanatory model of interest here is its relationship with notions of conspiracy and cover-up. The GWS explanatory system is layered in that it deals with chains of causation. It is also a moral system in that it makes sense of responsibility and enables the sufferer clearly to appoint blame. The GWS system is flexible, able to incorporate a huge variety of internal difference: different experiences; divergent symptoms; a magnitude of often-contradictory theories. It is adaptable, able to incorporate and encompass new findings and directions. But it is also a closed and watertight system, in that it deflects criticism and is able to respond to information that looks to contradict it. At the heart of veterans' world-view is that they were the objects of a medical conspiracy that continues to plague them. For the veteran the world is divided into black and white, as is the world of medicine and science: those that are with them and those who are against.

GWS illness narratives provide a template, a way to construct inclusive biographical narratives. It would appear that people reach for explanations that tie up loose ends and are able to incorporate a wide variety of experiences: people are struggling to construct a meta-narrative. Tied in to this process, particularly in regards to GWS, is the reliance on conspiracy theory. As Stewart (1999, p. 15) suggests, the details in one's experience create the need for a plot: 'It's not that for conspiracy theory everything is always already a rigid, all too clear, plot, but rather that the founding practice of conspiratorial thinking is the search for the missing plot. Think of it not as a prefabricated ideology…but as practice'. Furthermore, 'the system that makes sense of inchoate sensibilities and moments of strange convergence. It's practice born of a world that cries out for interpretation' (Stewart, 1999, p. 16). Conspiracy theory is a means of constituting reality where everything is connected and the connections are uncanny. In isolation, any one of these 'grains of salt' would not seem significant. GWS sufferers 'have not been provoked by any one traumatic or especially noteworthy incident. Instead, veterans have heard news stories, exchanged memos across the Internet, and, occasionally, met other vets with whom they could share stories. Theorization of conspiracy has thus been gradual, cumulative, and often via indirection' (Fortun, 1999, p. 346). Conspiracy theories in the GWS context have been 'provoked, produced, and made to function,' in order to respond to the strange and often contradictory information that circulates around the illness.

Conspiracy theory is nothing if not coherent, in fact 'the paranoid mentality is far more coherent than the real world since it leaves no room for mistakes, failures, or ambiguities' (Hofstadter, 1952, p. 36, in Marcus, 1999). The GWS diagnosis provides a template for meta-narrative that enables sufferers to link apparently disparate experiences into one, sweeping explanation. They give one the sense that everything is connected and explainable and that someone else is to blame. It makes the incoherent coherent.


## Either You Are Sick or You Are Sick in the Head

GWS explanatory models are linked to an overarching conspiracy theory: those that are against the veterans and those who support them (and their model of the illness). Those who are seen as being in opposition to the veterans are those who hold a conflicting theory of cause: one that is psychological or psychiatric in nature. The body/mind dichotomy that characterizes biomedical and psychiatric disease concepts does not represent objectively discoverable reality, but the philosophical foundation of a Western ethno-epistemology of health and illness that affords us little insight into affliction across a broad range of cultural contexts (Scheper-Hughes and Lock, 1987). Contested illnesses, such as GWS and CFS, highlight the limitations of this foundation. The debate regarding the impact of Gulf War exposures versus the psychosocial factors of the illness has tended to be oversimplified, emotive and highly polarized. The result of this is that research agendas, findings or positions are forced into black and white categories. Either you are for or you are against. Either the illness is physical or psychological.

Unfortunately, the result is that GWS sufferers are in a difficult position from which it is virtually impossible to escape, for how does one get better from an illness that remains unsolved and contested? How can one get better when one's very model of the illness is based on its chronicity and the notion of permanent damage? How does one move from striving for recognition and establishing the nature of the condition to one of therapy? For to get better at this point would expunge one's very understanding and conviction as to the nature of the illness. To a veteran suffering from GWS, recovery would, in many ways, be proving oneself and one's supporters wrong. Whilst conducting fieldwork, the author was struck by how rarely veterans spoke about treatment, seemingly suggesting that the illness was beyond recovery. This notion of GWS as chronic illness is linked to the veterans' explanatory model of their illness as a condition of irreversible depleted immunity and ongoing vulnerability.

Interviews with Gulf veterans were dominated by their focus on the immune system and its role in GWS theories. GWS sufferers almost universally see their illness as being caused by a weakened immune system caused by vaccinations and other exposures. Situating the illness in discussions of the immune system provides a biomedical and inclusive model for their suffering. Veterans draw upon themes and theories present in the world around them. In their discussions of the immune system they embed their understandings in widespread health beliefs, but they also can be seen as commenting upon their very unique experiences. People work with, negotiate and construct scientific knowledge and health beliefs. The concept of the immune system under assault and giving way under pressures of Twentieth-century life is a key idea in understanding illness beliefs at the end of the Twentieth century (Shorter, 1992; Wessely, 1997). We can see that the way GWS was being talked about and framed was influenced by popular understandings of illness.

There was widespread agreement amongst informants that the immune system was something contained within our bodies that protects us from disease. For most people, it is this system that determines whether one is going to get ill or remain well. Such findings reflect Martin's (1994) work, and as she states that it 'seems to follow from a robust notion of an internal system of protection that the system exists to ward off continual threats. People focus their attention on the well being of the system rather than on creating an environment that is free from threat' (p. 67). Veterans and those around them frequently express the notion that the environment surrounding our bodies contains many dangers that cannot be eliminated. Staying healthy is primarily about maintaining a strong immune system, but for sufferers of GWS, they see their immune systems as damaged and, thus, this defensive boundary is compromised. They are left vulnerable.

The immune system is central to the theories of causation of GWS, including severity of illness and infection rates. The illness involves a depleted immune system and the various specific illnesses and symptoms arise out of this deficiency. The immune system theory enables veterans to make a coherent, inclusive, system out of the incoherent. It provides explanations for a number of anomalies, such as why it is that the majority of veterans remain unaffected. For example, the veterans interviewed for this research explained that the majority of veterans had not become ill because they had stronger immune systems and that more may become ill as their immune systems naturally degraded with age. With the explanatory model being so focused on immune deficiency, the result is a theory of the illness that negates a process of recovery. For, if health is dependent upon having a healthy immune system that is able to ward off threats to health, then the veterans, who have an irrevocably diminished immune system, remain perennially under threat. It is not surprising that Gulf veterans, whose very suffering is in dispute, would look towards the immune system to organise and legitimate their illness, for the immune system has emerged 'as a field in terms of which all manner of questions and definitions about health are given meaning and measured' (Martin, 1994, p. xvii). Situating discussions of GWS enables veterans a medical language to describe their suffering whilst also reflecting lay perceptions of health. Simultaneously, understanding the illness as an illness of depleted immunity fits in with the desire to have an inclusive and flexible explanatory system.

## MEDICALISATION

The medicalisation of life, which has gathered pace in this century, tends to mean that distress is relocated from the social arena to the clinical arena, yet the costs may accrue for everyone over time if contributing factors rooted in political and commercial philosophies and practices escape proper scrutiny. One of the main aspects of the GWS narrative has been the push for medicalisation. The explanatory model held by veterans and their advocates is that the illness is a discrete, organic, disease involving the immune system, which was caused by Gulf exposures. They seek biomedical legitimacy and acknowledgement of their suffering. Veterans are pushing for a biomedical interpretation of their illness and have been somewhat successful in deflecting attention away from theories that may include psychological and social dimensions.

In accordance with the other contributors to this manuscript, the author suggests that there is a real problem with over-medicalisation of problems and the need to reduce unnecessary medical investigations. One of the major issues with medicalising problems is that it means we lose sight of the social dimensions of suffering: by translating social or economic issues into medical problems the complex social, personal, and physical causes of distress are lost. Anthropologists have also warned against the translation of metaphors of experience into reified biomedical entities (Scheper-Hughes and Lock, 1986). For distress is often expressed through somatic symptoms and somatising metaphors. Medicalisation entails missing the connection between the individual and social body and results in a tendency to transform the social to the biological (Scheper-Hughes and Lock, 1987). When symptoms get translated and reified into diseases we are no longer able to see them as statements and expressions of dis-ease. Scheper-Hughes's (1992) work on hunger in Brazil, for example, illustrated this process as she witnessed hunger being translated into an illness. The symptoms of hunger were no longer understood as a lack of food caused by extreme poverty, but instead as an illness of nerves. The result is that the origins of the symptoms (poverty, politics, the economic/social/historical order) were allowed to be ignored. Thus, the 'overproduction of illness in contemporary advanced industrial societies' ensures that the underlying social and political causes remain untouched (Scheper-Hughes and Lock, 1987, p. 27).

Illness can also be seen as resistance, as a form of protest. The 'individual body should be seen as the most immediate, the proximate terrain where social truths and social contradictions are played out, as well as a locus of personal and social resistance, creativity, and struggle' (Scheper-Hughes and Lock, 1987, p. 31). Medicalisation often means that the person disappears from the focus of inquiry as does their social context: the social origins of illness. All illnesses benefit from being approached holistically, but perhaps contested illnesses like GWS do so more. Illness narratives provide a framework for approaching a person's problems in a more holistic way and they can offer a method for addressing existential qualities not easily reached my other means, such as despair, grief, and moral pain, which often 'accompany, and may even constitute, people's illnesses' (Greenhalgh and Hurwitz, 1999, p. 48). Using a person's illness narrative and understanding the web of meanings associated with that illness provides a way to bring back these complex aspects of suffering.

Perhaps the greatest concern comes from the flip side of medicalisation: the ever-narrowing definitions of 'normal' that help turn the complaints of the healthy into the conditions of the sick (Moynihan, 2003). Connected to this process of medicalisation is the fact that, as social and other issues become medicalised, the only way to get treatment, help or legitimisation is through the medical system. Increasingly, all suffering is being medicalised and we are left with a situation where it is difficult to be accepted as suffering if your problem is not recognized medically. At the heart of this state of affairs is that suffering has been collapsed onto medical care. If you are suffering, then you are in need of medical care, 'if you then can't get medical care or insurance or disability, then there is an assumption that you probably aren't really sick and you probably aren't really suffering. It points, perhaps, to a cultural situation where we have become dependent on the verification of suffering by third parties' (Dumit, 2006, p. 585). Thus, if one is ill, but does not have a legitimate (medically defined illness) then you may just be a bit mad.

There has been a tendency, however, to simplify the process of medicalisation. Medicalisation has generally been thought of as the medical profession appropriating social problems to expand their domain of expertise and control (Nichter, 1980). Social scientists, however, have pointed out that medicalisation is more complex than this, for the construction of illness and the process of medicalisation is part of a dialogue between various forces. Medicalisation is not just of the medical profession and is not just about issues of control (Nichter, 1998), but is used by many people for a variety of reasons. Organizational pressures and bureaucratic systems often drive doctors to medicalise conditions (Daniels, 1969; Ingleby, 1982 in Nichter, 1998). The public's beliefs also compel clinicians to consider and label certain illnesses as medical entities. In the case of GWS, it is the veterans and their advocates who push for the medicalisation of their suffering, often against the opinion of the medical profession. As Nichter (1998) suggests, the medicalisation of a disorder 'may be self-initiated, engaged prior to medical confirmation or contrary to the opinion of doctors. Health-care seeking may be undertaken to legitimise and validate a sick role already assumed and enacted' (p.327).

Medicalisation in the GWS case is instigated by the sufferers themselves, but it is a particular kind of medicalisation, linked to the strong anti-psychiatry position of these illness movements. Correlated to their conviction that their illness is physical, they focus on the tools of medical science to uncover its mystery. GWS and other new illness movements are characterized by analogies of struggle and injustice. GWS literature remains highly critical of medicine and doctors, but it also espouses an extreme faith in the absolute success of medical science in unlocking the enigma of GWS. Shorter (1995) notes physicians are frequently described as 'heartless ignoramuses, blinkered in the cul-de-sac of mainline medicine.' In the GWS movement, doctors and scientists are valorised as excellent if their conclusions support the cause, yet demonised if they refute the presence of GWS. Doctors, however, remain the gatekeepers and veterans maintain an adamant belief in the power of medicine. Such movements attack medical authority at the same time as they desire its approval (Aronwitz, 1992). Thus, veterans demand more and more tests believing that one such test will eventually reveal the physical nature and cause of their suffering. They demand to be the object of medical science.

Their narratives are saturated with medical discourse. Veterans make use of scientists' theories and incorporate them into their explanatory models: they pick and choose, using parts of scientific theories, combining and changing them. Veterans' theories are a jumble of various strings, sometimes overlapping, sometimes held simultaneously, and often being altered. This system may look confused, but it is no different from how most people make sense of the world; people pick and choose those theories available to them to best make sense of their view of the world. It is a coherent system but it is also flexible. People build theories to make sense of their lives and these may not reflect the biomedical way of making sense of the world, yet veterans' theories remain very rooted in science and medical language. Veterans ignore, embrace, alter and accommodate various scientific findings and understandings about GWS and the world at large.

Lay participation in medical matters and the associated questioning of science is part of a larger cultural movement. Linked to the increase in health anxiety that we witness in the present cultural milieu (see below) is a general sense of uncertainty and a mistrust of science and scientists, and GWS is prime example of this process. The ' "objects" of scientisation also become the subjects of it, in the sense that they can and must actively manipulate the heterogeneous supply of scientific interpretations' (Beck, 1992, p. 157). This questioning of science and the accompanying process of picking and choosing from available scientific information characterizes GWS, yet this process can be seen as characteristic of the larger society in which GWS emerged. There is no scientific monopoly on discussions of risk as there is rarely expert agreement on what constitutes a risk, and how it might be managed. As a result, public uncertainty increases, as does criticism. Think of the MMR debate that emerged due, in part, to conflicting notions of risk within the scientific community and an accompanying mistrust of doctors, scientists and the government. Knowledge is contested between lay and scientists, but also between scientists. People are increasingly sceptical of what scientists have to say, and use their own experiences or those around them to fill in the gaps. In new illness movements it is the sufferers themselves who are seen as the experts. They are experts by the nature of their experience. As Shorter (1992) noted, the theme of medical incompetence and indifference runs through the CFS movement 'which elevates the patients' subjective knowledge of their bodies to the same status as the doctors' objective knowledge. This presumption of privileged self- knowledge of one's body dovetails perfectly with media marketing strategies' (p. 317).

Similarly, in the Gulf case, expertise is held by veterans' own knowledge of their bodies and experiences, but they seek more and more scientific knowledge to increase their expertise. Due, in part, to the way the GWS debate has developed, veterans find themselves conversing in often extremely complicated medical language. In order to strengthen their claim to expertise they often claim proficiency in medical matters saying, for example that 'many veterans are medically trained'. Interestingly, many of the leaders of the associations and the GWS movement overall who claim such medical expertise and, in so doing are seen as the ultimate authority due to their individual experience, gained scientific knowledge through studying the case and medical background. The recent appointment of two doctors onto the board of one of the support groups is further evidence of this push to claim medical knowledge. Although they stress their knowledge of medical theories, they also defer to their supporters within the medical and scientific community and they, too are seen as GWS experts.

During interviews with Gulf veterans one of the themes that emerged was the notion of GWS being invisible. Veterans often spoke of their frustration of having an illness that was not obvious or visible and, thus, they were caught in a cycle of always having to prove how ill they were. If life for a GWS sufferer is geared towards the recognition of being ill, what does this mean for getting better? Alexander (1982) has described the 'new American sick role', where those who are ill are compensated for their illness and have little reason to give it up. People often have an investment in being ill and in seeing their problem as a medical condition. Medicalisation, indeed, is their way of coping with suffering. Medicalisation may constitute a strategy to deal with suffering through the construction of a narrative to make sense out of chaotic life events that threaten one's sense of self-integrity (Cassel, 1982).

The medicalisation drive characterizes the present Euro-American milieu and is often driven upwards from below. People are increasingly bothered by, aware of, and disabled by, distress and discomforts. Society's 'heightened consciousness of health has led to greater self-scrutiny and an amplified awareness of bodily symptoms and feelings of illness', whilst the widespread 'commercialization of health and the increasing focus on health issues in the media have created a climate of apprehension, insecurity, and alarm about disease' (Barsky, 1988, p. 414). GWS and other new illnesses 'often assume prominence in the mass communications media and public consciousness before their scientific dimensions have been established' (Barsky and Borus, 1995, p. 1932). It would seem that every day life is saturated with anxiety about the world around us. Every day there is another health scare about which to worry.

Acting in accordance with the Euro-American worldview, the veterans studied here were likely to view symptoms as pathological and interpret them medically. We automatically think of somatic discomfort and symptoms as expressions of organic pathology. The popular belief is that the physical world is a potentially hostile and toxic place that erodes health and well-being. The tendency to conceptualise medical problems in biological terms is powerful, and medical practitioners are often reluctant to explore the non-biological aspects of a patient's case, as are many patients. Patients respond to the cues offered by health professionals and are themselves part of a culture that continues to stigmatise mentally ill people and those with emotional problems. As a result of this 'potential stigma, patients are naturally eager to avoid psychiatric labelling and seek a medical or other external, environmental explanation for their distress' (Kirmayer, 1999, p. 274). We are less tolerant of aches and pains; we actively worry about symptoms and pay attention to them. Because of the heightened scrutiny of health we have become prone to health scares, to blaming 'allergens', toxins, chemicals and viruses for failures and unhappiness. Anything that falls outside complete health and happiness is not tolerated and needs an explanation. It needs a cause and by uncovering cause we uncover who is to blame. The public at large increasingly seeks medical solutions to life's problems. Gulf veterans can be seen as experiencing a kind of Twentieth/Twenty-first century malaise that is at the heart of most new illness movements. Like the majority of people, veterans are likely to seek out a medical explanation for their sense of malaise, misfortune and unravelling. For Gulf veterans, however, there is a well-documented, well-advertised, illness within easy reach.

Correlated to the process of medicalisation is the tendency to subject patients to a high level of physical examinations and tests, and this can increase concern. Paying 'increased attention to one's body and one's health tends to make one assess them more negatively, with greater feelings of ill health' (Barsky, 1988, p. 416). Research has revealed that bodily awareness, self-consciousness, and introspection are associated with a tendency to amplify somatic symptoms and to report being troubled by more symptoms (Mechanic, 1983; Miller *et al.*, 1981; Pennebaker, 1982). The more aware people are of their characteristics and attributes, the more negatively they assess them (Pennebaker, 1982), and this appears to be particularly true for physical attributes, bodily sensations, and perceptions of health (Barsky, 1988). The types of test that are done may also feed specific notions of cause. Focusing on imunological tests, for example, will likely strengthen a patient's belief that their illness is one of the immune system and may be seen as support of their perspective. Again this is associated with the way the illness has been constructed and led by lay beliefs about causation.

## The Media

As mentioned above, the media play a dominant role in the process of medicalisation. The role of the media in the construction of this syndrome, by disseminating information and adding validation to certain assumptions and tropes, is central to the development of GWS. Almost all informants for this research reported that whilst they felt 'not themselves', they did not realize what was wrong with them until they saw or heard a media report about GWS. The media have also played a large role in the presentation of information and the negotiation of knowledge and expertise. The GWS story and the way it has been presented in the media have caused a great deal of anxiety amongst 'well' veterans. Although many well Gulf War veterans remained somewhat sceptical of the illness, the vast majority of them remained worried that one day they may come down with unexplainable illnesses. It has also caused a great deal of anxiety amongst serving military personnel. Increasingly it is the media, not the medical profession that is the ultimate arbiter of what constitutes a 'real' disease (Shorter, 1995) and what is considered 'real' science. Personal testimonies of GWS are often taken as the most authentic truth, with media reports relying on personal stories. Inquiries, such as the Lord Lloyd inquiry and the House of Lords forum, were dependent upon the personal testimonies of sufferers whilst the voices of scientists and doctors were almost entirely absent.

## CONCLUSIONS

GWS is wider than the Gulf War and GWS is about much more than itself. Illnesses are innately cultural and, thus, understanding veterans' health problems requires sensitivity to the wider context of their lives. Most informants had left the military soon after the Gulf War and so GWS seems to have a great deal to do with an unsuccessful move from military to civilian life. Sufferers appeared to struggle in producing a satisfactory identity and a consistency with identity as a soldier. Ascribing to a GWS provides meaning and anchoring for a struggling veteran. It also provides membership of a community of sufferers who share many of their experiences. Striving to uncover a unitary cause is not the answer – illness is much more complicated than that. Whereas the discourse surrounding GWS has focused on proving that it is either a physical or psychiatric condition, it may be more helpful to understand it as neither physical nor psychological, but both. Simultaneously, it is a social and cultural condition. A helpful approach to understanding GWS and other post-combat syndromes is that of interpreting them as an idiom of distress: a way to express and communicate suffering. Certain symptoms and symptom reporting that may not be medically or epidemiologically relevant, are extremely relevant to sufferers and are conveying meaning. It is pertinent to comprehend an individual's explanatory model and accounts of their illness in order to work with them and reach consensus. Although we increasingly look to medicine to legitimise suffering, GWS reveals that medicalising a problem may, in the end, prove harmful. Gulf veterans are caught in a double bind: they struggle to 'prove' the biomedical reality of their suffering and this leaves them both dissatisfied and unable to gain satisfactory help. Veterans' understanding of their illness is built upon notions of being wronged and harmed by their government and this ill-treatment, they feel, continues at the hands of a medical system that refutes their illness model; this makes them extremely difficult to engage in any move towards therapy.

Furthermore, their explanatory model is constructed around a theory of irreparably damaged immunity. Both of these elements of their perception of their illness put them in a liminal position where recovery is unlikely.

# REFERENCES

Alexander, L. (1982). Illness maintenance and the new American sick role, in *Clinically Applied Anthropology*, N.J. Chrisman and T.W.W. Marezki (Eds), Dordrecht, Holland: Reidel Publishing, pp. 351–66.

Aronowitz, R. (1992). From myalgic encephalitis to yuppie flu: a history of chronic fatigue syndrome, in *Framing Disease*, C. Rosenberg and J.Golden (Eds), New Brunswick: Rutgers University Press, pp. 155–181.

Barsky, A. (1988). The paradox of health, *New England Journal of Medicine*, 414–418.

Barsky, A. and Borus, J. (1995). Somatization and medicalization in the era of managed care, *Journal of the American Medical Association*, **274**, 1931–1934.

Beck (1991).

Beck, U. (1992). *Risk Society*, London: Sage.

Boyd, K., Hallman, W., Wartenberg, D., Fielder, N., Brewer, N. and Kipen, H. (2004). Reported exposures, stressors, and life events among Gulf War registry veterans, *Journal of Occupational and Environmental Medicine*, **45**, 1247–1256.

Cassel, E. (1982). The nature of suffering and the goals of medicine, *New England Journal of Medicine*, **306**, 639–45.

Chalder, T., Hull, L., Unwin, C., David, A., Hotopf, M. and Wessely, S. (2001). Prevalence of Gulf war veterans who think they have Gulf War Syndrome, *British Medical Journal*, **323**, 473–476.

Daniels, D. (1969). The captive professional: bureaucratic limitations in the practice of military psychiatry, *Journal of Health and Social Behaviour*, **10**, 222–65.

Douglas, M. (1970). *Natural Symbols*, New York: Vantage Press.

DiGiacomo, S. (1992). Metaphor as illness: postmodern dilemmas in the representation of body, mind and disorder, *Medical Anthropology*, **14**, 109–37.

Dumit, J. (2006). Illnesses you have to fight to get: facts and forces in uncertain, emergent illnesses, *Social Science and Medicine*, **62**, 577–590

Eisenberg (1981), cited in Garro and Mattingly (2000).

Ewart, C., Stewart, K., Gillilan, R., *et al.* (1986). Usefulness of self-efficacy in predicting overexertion during programmed excercise in coronary artery disease, *American Journal of Cardiology*, **57**, 557–561.

Fortun, K. (1999). Lone Gunmen: Legacies of the Gulf War Illness, and unseen enemies, in *Paranoia Within Reason: a Casebook on Conspiracy as Explanation*, G. Marcus (Ed.), Chicago: University of Chicago Press, pp. 343–373.

Garro, L. and Mattingly, C. (2000). Narrative as construct and construction, in *Narrative and the Cultural Construction of Illness and Healing*, C. Mattingly, and L. Garro (Eds.), Berkeley: University of California Press, pp.1–49

Giddens, A. (1991). *Modernity and Self Identity*, Cambridge: Polity Press.

Good, B. (1977). The heart of what's the matter: the semantics of illness in iran, *Culture, Medicine and Psychiatry*, **1**, 25–58.

Gray, G. and Kang, H. (2006). Healthcare utilisation and mortality among veterans of the Gulf War, *Philosophical Transactions of the Royal Society*, **361**, 553–570.

Greenhalgh, T. and Hurwitz, B. (1999). Why study narrative? *British Medical Journal*, **318**, 48–50.

Hofstadter, R. (1952, 1967). *The Paranoid Style in American Politics and Other Essays*, New York: Random House.

Hunt, S., Richardson, R., Engel, C., Atkins, D. and McFall, M. (2004). Gulf War veterans' illnesses: A pilot study of the relationship between illness beliefs to symptom severity and functional health status, *Journal of Occupational and Environmental Medicine*, **46**, 818–827.

Ingleby, D. (1982). The social construction of mental illness, in *The Problem of Medical Knowledge: Examining the Social Construction of Medicine*, P. Wright and A. Treacher (Eds). Edinburgh: University of Edinburgh Press.

Ismail, K. and Lewis, G. (2006). Multi-symptom illnesses, unexplained illness and Gulf War Syndrome, *Philosophical Transactions of the Royal Society B*, **361**, 543–551.

Kilshaw, S. (2004). Friendly fire: the construction of Gulf War syndrome narratives, *Anthropology and Medicine*, **11**, 149–160.

Kirmayer, L. (1996). Confusion of the senses: implications of cultural variations in somatoform and dissociative disorders for PTSD, in *Ethnocultural Aspects of Post-Traumatic Stress Disorders*, A. Marsella, M. Friedman, E. Garrity and R. Scurfield (Eds). Washington DC: American Psychological Press.

Kirmayer, L. (1999). Rhetorics of the Body: Medically Unexplained Symptoms in Socio-cultural Perspective, in *Somatoform Disorders: A Worldwide Perspective*, Y. Ono, A. Janca, M. Asai, and N. Sartorius (Eds). Tokyo; Springer.

Kirmayer, L. and Young, A. (1988). Culture and somatization: clinical, epidemiological and ethnographic perspectives, *Psychosomatic Medicine*, **60**, 420–430.

Kleinman, A., and Kleinman, J. (1991). Suffering and its professional transformation: toward an ethnography of interpersonal experience, *Culture, Medicine and Psychiatry*, **15**, 275–301.

Marcus, G. (Ed.) (1999). *Paranoia Within Reason: A Casebook on Conspiracy as Explanation*. Chicago: University of Chicago Press.

Martin, E. (1994). *Flexible Bodies: Tracking Immunity in American Culture from Days of Polio to the Age of AIDS*, Boston: Beacon Press.

Mechanic, D. (Ed.) (1983). *Handbook of Health, Health Care, and the Health Professions*, New York: Free Press, pp. 591–607.

Melucci, A. (1989). *Nomads of the Present: Social Movements and Individual Needs in Contemporary Society*, Philadelphia: Temple University Press.

Melucci, A. (1996a). *Challenging Codes: Collective Action in the Information Age*, Cambridge: Cambridge University Press.

Melucci, A. (1996b). *The Playing Self: Person and Meaning in a Planetary Society*. Cambridge, UK: Cambridge University Press.

Miller, L.C., Murphy, R., Buss, A.H. (1981). Consciousness of body: private and public, *Journal of Personality and Social Psychology*, **41**, 397–406.

Moynihan, R. (2003). The making of a disease: female sexual dysfunction, *British Medical Journal*, **326**, 45–47.

Nichter, M. (1980). The layperson's perception of medicine as perspective into the utilisation of multiple therapy systems in the Indian context, *Social Science and Medicine*, **14B**, 225–233.

AN ANTHROPOLOGICAL APPROACH TO GWS

Nichter, M. (1981). Idioms of distress: alternatives in the expression of psychosocial distress, a South Indian case study, *Culture, Medicine and Psychiatry*, 1, 9–23.

Nichter, M. (1998). The mission within the madness: self–initiated medicalization as expression of agency, in *Pragmatic Women and Body Politics*, M. Lock and P. Kaufert (Eds), Cambridge: Cambridge University Press, pp. 327–353.

Obeyesekere, G. (1981). *Medusa's Hair: An Essay on Personal Symbols and Religious Experience*, Chicago: University of Chicago Press.

Obeyesekere, G. (1985). Buddhism, depression and the work of culture in Sri Lanka, in *Culture and Depression*, A. Kleinman and B. Good (Eds), Berkeley, Calif.: University of California Press, pp. 134–152.

Obeyesekere, G. (1990). *The Work of Culture: Symbolic Transformation in Psychoanalysis and Anthropology*, Chicago and London: University of Chicago Press.

Pennebaker, J.W. (2003). Telling stories: the health benefits of disclosure, in *Social and Cultural Lives of Immune Systems*, J. Wilce (Ed.) London, UK: Routledge.

Pennebaker, J.W. (1982). *The Psychology of Physical Symptoms*, New York: Springer–Verlag.

Reid, J. and Reynold, L. (1990). Requiem for RSI: the explanation and control of an occupational epidemic, *Medical Anthropology Quarterly*, 4, 162–190.

Scheper–Hughes, N. (1992). *Death Without Weeping: The Violence of Everyday Life in Brazil*. Berkeley: University of California Press.

Scheper–Hughes, N. and Lock (1986). Speaking 'truth' to illness: Metaphors, reification, and a pedagogy for patients, *Medical Anthropology Quarterly*, 17(5), 137–140.

Scheper–Hughes, N. and Lock (1987). The mindful body: a prologemenon to future work in medical anthropology, *Medical Anthropology Quarterly*, 1, 6–41.

Sensky, T. (1997). Causal attributions in physical illness, *Journal of Psychosomatic Research*, 43, 565–573.

Shorter, E. (1992). *From Paralysis to Fatigue: A History of Psychosomatic Illness in the Modern Era*, New York: The Free Press.

Shorter, E. (1995). Sucker punched again! Physicians meet the disease-of-the-month syndrome, *Journal of Psychosomatic Research*, 39, 115–188

Showalter, E. (1997). *Hystories: Hysterical Epidemics and Modern Culture*, New York: Columbia University Press.

Shriver, T., Webb, G. and Adams, B. (2002). Environmental exposures, contested illness, and collective action: the controversy over Gulf War Illness, *Humboldt Journal of Social Relations*, 27, 73–105.

Skultans, V. (2000). *Anthropology and Medicine*, 7(1), 5–13.

Spence (1982). In Garro and Mattingly (2000).

Stacey, J. (1997). *Teratologies: A Cultural Study of Cancer*, London: Routledge.

Stewart, K. (1999). Conspiracy theory's worlds, in *Paranoia Within Reason: A Casebook on Conspiracy as Explanation*, G. Marcus (Ed.), Chicago: University of Chicago Press, pp.13–20.

Ware, N. (1993). Society, mind and body in chronic fatigue syndrome: an anthropological view, in *Chronic Fatigue Syndrome*, G. Bock and J. Whelan (Eds), Chichester: John Wiley & Sons.

Wessely, S. (1997). Chronic Fatigue Syndrome: a 20th century illness? *Scandinavian Journal of Work and Environmental Health*, 23 (suppl. 3), 17–34.

Young, A. (1982). The anthropologies of illness and sickness, *Annual Review of Anthropology*, 11, 257–285.

# 5

# Combat Stress (The Ex-Services Mental Welfare Society), Veterans and Psychological Trauma

Keron Fletcher

## INTRODUCTION

Approximately 25 000 individuals leave the armed forces each year, and over the last 20 years 700 000 men and women have been discharged from military duties. Using the broadest definition of a veteran (that of having served one day in the armed forces) there are 5.5 million people who meet that criterion in the UK today, with an additional 7.5 million dependents. Unlike some Western nations, the United Kingdom does not have a veterans' medical service. When a serviceman is discharged from military service, he or she is expected to make use of free medical facilities provided by the National Health Service (NHS).

Most individuals leaving the armed forces have enjoyed and benefited from their experiences and are successful in obtaining subsequent employment. However, within the overall population of veterans there are wide variations of need. Among the most vulnerable ex–servicemen

*War and Health: Lessons from the Gulf War*   Edited by Harry Lee & Edgar Jones
© 2007 John Wiley & Sons, Ltd

and women are those in prison (4–5 % of the prison population), those who are homeless (25 % of single homeless people) and those with mental health problems.

The most commonly identified psychiatric disorders seen in UK veterans are depression, anxiety, post-traumatic stress disorder (PTSD) and alcohol disorders. Two or more diagnoses frequently occur together – of those with PTSD for example, 75 % have more than one diagnosis. There may be a tendency for PTSD to be over-diagnosed by civilian medical practitioners assessing veterans. This may be due to the complexity of such assessments, or because PTSD is easily recognised as being precipitated by trauma whereas the other conditions are not. Conversely, however, by the time veterans seek the help of specialist organisations they not infrequently have already received diagnoses of anxiety, depression or alcohol dependence but PTSD has been missed.

# COMBAT STRESS (THE EX–SERVICES MENTAL WELFARE SOCIETY)

Combat Stress is a charity, founded on 1st June 1918. With the sole exception of the NHS it is the only agency of any size in Britain that is dedicated to addressing the complex needs of veterans with mental health problems. Until recently its remit has been to assist the return to work of ex-servicemen and women through a programme of residential care, rehabilitation and training. In the last 15 years, the focus of the Society's intervention has changed, so that there is now a stronger emphasis on the treatment of traumatic psychological reactions. Although the NHS treats various degrees of disorder in many veterans, it lacks the specialised resources to engage effectively in the long term with some of the most difficult cases that involve social disenfranchisement, psychological trauma, complex combinations of physical and psychiatric illness and high levels of substance misuse and dependence. Therefore, individuals who present to Combat Stress tend to have more severe and chronic difficulties than the majority of veterans who are treated within the NHS.

Table 5.1 lists the fields of conflict in which individuals receiving treatment with Combat Stress served. Many veterans served in more than one theatre. The psychiatric casualty rate for each field of conflict

Table 5.1   Numbers of patients from each field of conflict

| Field of conflict | Number of active cases | % |
|---|---|---|
| Northern Ireland | 1055 | 33 |
| World War 2 | 437 | 14 |
| Gulf War 1 | 354 | 11 |
| Falkland Islands | 284 | 9 |
| Balkans | 166 | 5 |
| Aden | 119 | 4 |
| Cyprus | 108 | 3 |
| Malaya | 74 | 2 |
| Korea | 54 | 1.5 |
| Non-conflict trauma | 381 | 12 |
| Other war zones | 168 | 5.5 |

is not known, but the proportion of war pension awards for psychiatric illness has stayed more or less constant at 8–10 % since 1919:

Combat Stress provides care in two ways:

(i) Community–based welfare support services are provided nation-wide by a team of Regional Welfare Officers.

(ii) Short-term treatment is provided by a team of nurses, other therapists and visiting ex-military consultant psychiatrists (who have specialised knowledge of military culture and the impact of conflict) at three residential treatment units (two in England and one in Scotland).

## Welfare support services

Referrals to Combat Stress are received by three regional welfare departments situated at each of the residential treatment centres. Self-referrals account for most of the referrals received (35 %), the majority of others coming from services that support military or ex-military personnel. These include:

• War Pensions Welfare Service (16.4 %);
• Soldiers, Sailors, Airmen and Families Association (SSAFA, 8.5 %);
• Royal British Legion (5.9 %);
• NHS medical services such as general gractitioners (GPs) or psychiatrists (3.9 %), community mental health teams (3.7 %);
• Gulf Veterans Medical Assessment Programme (0.8 %);
• benevolent funds of the three services;

- regimental associations;
- other agencies including the probation pervice, Relate, Citizens Advice Bureau, local councils and housing associations.

The average period from military discharge to referral to Combat Stress is a lengthy 14.1 years, with veterans having served a mean of 11.1 years. Barriers to obtaining help include the stigma attached to mental health problems, military ethos, NHS mental health services that are configured to prioritise severe enduring mental illness, and problems for veterans in engaging with treatment services that have little understanding of military culture or combat-related psychological trauma.

A total of 12 regional welfare officers provide the community component of care. They are all ex-service officers with first-hand experience of warfare or conflict. Their work with veterans starts with an initial assessment, which can be conducted in a variety of settings. Most commonly this takes place in an individual's home, but if necessary other venues such as nursing homes, hospitals, prisons, motorway service stations, supermarket cafes and even hilltops have been used. At present there is a demand for 750–800 new assessments annually. Severely affected veterans do not find it easy to discuss their experiences within normal civilian settings for reasons mentioned above, and frequently hide their symptoms and difficulties from close relatives and GPs. The welfare officer's initial assessment is, therefore, not uncommonly the first occasion when veterans disclose traumatic memories.

Following the initial assessment, welfare officers remain in contact with veterans through home visits, telephone calls, attendance at various group meetings and during periods of residential treatment. Efforts are made to meet with other family members for the purposes of obtaining additional information and to provide support and advice. A welfare officer is able to refer veterans to the three residential treatment centres run by Combat Stress.

Welfare officers conduct approximately 500 visits per annum, carry a caseload of 400 veterans and travel 30 000 miles per year in the course of their duties. Relevant information about psychological disorders is documented in a comprehensive assessment report and passed on to nursing and medical staff at the three Combat Stress residential treatment centres.

The most common psychological and social problems described to Welfare Officers at first assessment are listed in Tables 5.2 and 5.3 (not in order of frequency):

**Table 5.2**   Psychological symptoms

| Psychological symptoms |
| --- |
| Nightmares |
| Flashbacks |
| Suicidal thoughts |
| Disturbed sleep |
| Anxiety |
| Anger |
| Mood swings |
| Bitterness |
| Poor concentration |
| Guilt |
| Forgetfulness |
| Depression |
| Low self-esteem |
| Hopelessness |

**Table 5.3**   Social problems

**Social problems**

Housing:

- Homelessness
- Poor conditions
- Inappropriate housing
- Tenancy/financial problems
- Need for aids and adaptations for older clients

Employment difficulties or unemployment
Financial difficulties
War pension problems
Legal problems
Other miscellaneous difficulties, e.g.:

- Marital relationships
- Lone parent problems
- Access to children

# Social Welfare Problems

Welfare officers address the social problems facing veterans by giving information and advice, assisting with practical planning and problem solving, by drawing on the assistance of other agencies or through onward referral.

Between 20–25 % of homeless people living rough on the streets of London are ex-servicemen or women (SSAFA–Forces Help website). Some veterans have been known to live in tents, garden sheds or other run-down or squalid conditions. These circumstances usually arise due to failure to pay rent or council tax, and may often be associated with substance misuse or mental health problems.

Less than one third of individuals assessed by welfare officers are in paid employment. Frequently these veterans have a poor employment record after leaving military service, arising from a failure to adjust to civilian working patterns, or due to mental health problems. Debts are therefore common, and exacerbated by ignorance of entitlements to state benefits or a war pension (for those with psychiatric or physical disorders attributable to military service). Fewer than 10 % of veterans assessed by Combat Stress welfare officers have a war pension, although the assessments suggest that the majority qualify for one.

Most legal problems are related to heavy alcohol consumption and episodes of violence. Aggressive behaviour may be triggered by combat-related memories and is often an important factor that also underlies self-harm or attempted suicide.

## RESIDENTIAL TREATMENT CENTRES

Combat Stress has three residential treatment centres, providing approximately 2500 admissions annually. They are: (i) Tyrwhitt House – Leatherhead, Surrey; (ii) Audley Court – Newport, Shropshire, and (iii) Hollybush House – Ayr, Scotland.

Each treatment centre is staffed by registered mental nurses, supported by other therapists. They deliver treatments with the guidance and support of visiting psychiatrists. Two of the current three visiting psychiatrists are ex-military consultant psychiatrists. General medical support is provided through local health centres and out-of-hours services if required.

A visiting medical officer would be struck by a number of common features of Combat Stress clinics. There is a marked variety of clinical presentations, with chronic physical disease or injury co-existing with chronic mental illness, psychological trauma, substance-misuse disorders, personality disorders and serious social problems. Most of the patients become distressed when recounting their military experiences. PTSD is still active and distressing in patients who have had symptoms for 50 years or more. The diagnosis was often made many years after the onset of the disorder, and in these cases a subsequent stressor, often relatively minor, commonly appears to have precipitated an acute decompensation that led to the diagnosis. The age range of patients is wide, from late teens through to late 80s, and, unsurprisingly, males make up 97 % of the client group.

The complexity of cases admitted to treatment centres is illustrated in Table 5.4, which shows six main health areas affecting 100 patients seen at clinics in Shropshire and Ayrshire.

For each individual, the mean number of areas affected was 4.4, with psychological trauma being the single most common problem.

Psychotropic drug prescribing is heavy in this group of patients as shown below in Table 5.5. Even making allowances for some poor prescribing practices, the data demonstrates how difficult it can be for GPs or psychiatric services to manage the severe and complex psychiatric problems presented by this patient group. Forty-four per cent of patients are prescribed two or more psychotropic drugs.

It is difficult to grade the severity of each individual case, as severity can refer to the degree of distress, the number of symptoms, the degree of dysfunction, the type of presenting disorder or the severity of the

Table 5.4  Principal health areas

| 1<br>Physical<br>illness<br>(%) | 2<br>Physical<br>trauma<br>(%) | 3<br>Psychiatric<br>illness<br>(%) | 4<br>Psychological<br>trauma<br>(%) | 5<br>Past or present<br>problem with<br>alcohol or<br>drugs (%) | 6<br>Significant<br>social<br>difficulty in<br>childhood or<br>adolescence<br>(%) |
|---|---|---|---|---|---|
| 75 | 68 | 75 | 94 | 74 (71 %<br>alcohol,<br>3 % illicit<br>drugs) | 50 |

Table 5.5  Number of psychotropic drugs prescribed

| Number of psychotropic drugs prescribed | % |
|---|---|
| 0 | 22 |
| 1 | 38 |
| 2 | 23 |
| 3 | 12 |
| 4 | 3 |
| 5 | 2 |

management difficulties. Using a very basic clinical grading system, with the assessing clinician recording an impression of the severity of all of the above factors, ratings were made on 100 consecutive medical assessments. These are shown in Table 5.6, where:

- 'Simple' problems were those in which the presenting difficulties were related to psychological trauma alone.
- 'Complex' problems refers to psychological trauma plus other significant problems, such as physical illness or injury, addictive disorder, or problems in childhood and adolescence that were considered to have adversely affected coping skills development.
- 'Moderate' grade reflects the severity of the average patient seen within a Combat Stress setting. It is important to appreciate that less experienced practitioners would probably consider this degree of difficulty to be severe.

Several cases are briefly described towards the end of this chapter that will illustrate the use of the grading system.

A number of patterns emerge as histories are gathered from these veterans. As mentioned above, it is usual for memories of past war-related events to be recounted with great distress, despite many years or even decades having passed since the precipitating trauma. Hypervigilant behaviour persists in some men, so that they will not, for instance, sit with their back to a door during a clinical interview. The most frequently described troublesome symptoms described by patients undergoing residential treatment are nightmares and sleep disturbance. As a result of these difficulties married men may not sleep in the same bed as their wives, due to restlessness, shouting or even episodes of violence that occur during sleep or upon waking from a nightmare. Unmarried men may deliberately avoid forming sexual relationships, as they do not want their partners to be subjected to their aggression or episodic violence. Many veterans, due to a sense of danger or threat, find it difficult to leave their homes and therefore live isolated and solitary lives.

Table 5.6  Severity grading

| No treatment required (%) | Mild, simple problems (%) | Moderate, simple problems (%) | Severe, simple problems (%) | Moderate, complex problems (%) | Severe, complex problems (%) |
|---|---|---|---|---|---|
| 4 | 1 | 10 | 6 | 69 | 10 |

Veterans seen in residential treatment centres very strongly express the view that they wish to be treated with other ex-military personnel. Civilian medical services are often criticised for failing to understand their particular needs and expectations. It is important for treating staff to have credibility with veterans. It is one of the particular advantages of Combat Stress that many of the staff have served in the armed forces or have extensive experience of working with ex-servicemen and women. Veterans frequently report feeling 'safe', being able to relax in this setting. This is in contrast to life at home, where they are usually hypervigilant and on edge.

## TREATMENT APPROACHES

Combat Stress has a broad remit to provide care for veterans with mental health problems. This is especially for combat-related psychological disorders, but not exclusively so. Support is also provided for the relatively small numbers of individuals with severe mental illnesses such as schizophrenia or manic-depressive psychosis, whether or not these conditions occur in association with PTSD. On occasions it is not possible to provide therapeutic interventions for PTSD due to the presence of dementia, head injury with short-term memory impairment, or acute psychosis. Management of PTSD is commonly complicated by the presence of substance misuse disorders. The present level of on-site medical and nursing cover does not permit the admission of acutely suicidal patients, or patients who suffer severe alcohol withdrawal symptoms involving fits or delirium tremens. Alcohol dependence is the most common diagnosis occurring together with PTSD, but it is noticeable that increasing numbers of young ex-servicemen are now presenting with dependence on illicit drugs.

Nearly all (94 %) of the veterans seen at Combat Stress residential treatment centres have some form of psychological reaction to a traumatic event. The diagnosis is usually PTSD acquired during service in the armed forces. For some of the most vulnerable and severely affected individuals with PTSD, any treatment involving exposure to triggers or memories of the traumatic event cannot be given. The exacerbation of symptoms precipitated by this approach can lead to a period of unmanageable distress, associated with suicidal or homicidal threats, self-harm or substance misuse. In these cases approaches are adopted that aim to improve the quality of life by focusing on other problems such as mood disorders, substance misuse or dependence, social isolation, unemployment or housing difficulties.

For the majority of individuals who are able to engage in active treatments for PTSD, three approaches are commonly used:

(i) Interventions are offered that reduce levels of anxiety or stress, such as relaxation exercises, anxiety management or anger management. This early phase of treatment is usually accompanied by education about PTSD to achieve a degree of 'normalization', so that veterans see their disorder as an understandable reaction to extreme and abnormal events rather than as a form of mental illness or madness;

(ii) Avoidance behaviours are identified, and graded behavioural exercises initiated to slowly build up the individual's ability and confidence in coping with situations they cannot normally tolerate;

(iii) The traumatic event that precipitated PTSD is revisited. Initially, methods that help to detach the individual emotionally from the trauma are used, such as producing collages or other artwork that expresses the trauma visually, or re-enacting the traumatic event with models. Gradually the veteran is encouraged to talk about the traumatic event, in increasing detail and with an increasing degree of emotional involvement. Sometimes a verbal account is recorded onto tape so that it can be listened to frequently. The rationale of this approach is the same as that of treating any phobic disorder – assuming that PTSD resembles, at least to some degree, a phobia to a memory, then repeated and graded exposure to the memory should eventually lead to extinction of the fear associated with it. During this phase of treatment there are opportunities to use cognitive techniques to modify distorted patterns of thinking (such as guilt for failing to act heroically, for surviving, or for causing death) often associated with extreme feelings of guilt or self-loathing. Approaches such as Eye Movement Desensitisation and Reprocessing (EMDR) that can accelerate the above process are used in suitable cases.

A frequently encountered problem in this sort of work is that patients do not want or expect to be distressed by the process of treatment. Inexperienced therapists also find it difficult to use approaches that precipitate horrific memories and intense feelings of distress. In these situations there is, therefore, a common tendency to allow treatment to drift towards therapies that provide symptomatic relief, but do not address the underlying traumatic disorder. Regular supervision and support is important and necessary for staff to be able to sustain the focus of treatment and to cope with the emotional demands made of them. Nursing and treating such patients on a day-to-day basis is extremely demanding, and this sort of work inevitably takes its toll on some members of staff.

The role of the visiting medical officer includes supporting nursing staff, assessing complex mental health problems, and corresponding with other medical services regarding medication for PTSD or health care for other clinical conditions. Other in-patient hospital facilities may, rarely, be needed if a veteran develops serious physical or psychiatric problems during treatment.

## CLINICAL OUTCOMES

Routine use of standardised assessment instruments has been introduced to all residential treatment centres to enhance the collection of outcome data. The data currently available is limited to assessment of the impact of a single admission. This data, collected from several hundred veterans across the residential treatment centres, shows a halving of scores on the GHQ 28 (General Health Questionnaire – 28 items) at the end of admission compared with the beginning of admission (mean score at beginning of admission = 12.2; mean score at end of admission = 5.9). The reductions were as follows:

Somatic symptoms – 45.4 %
Anxiety and Insomnia – 54.0 %
Social dysfunction – 55.0 %
Depression – 51.9 %
Total symptom reduction – 51.4 %

This level of improvement supports the view expressed by veterans that their lives at home are generally stressful and that they can relax and benefit from this particular therapeutic setting. However, these gains are usually temporary, with veterans reporting that benefits wear off over the weeks and months following their stay. It is necessary to note that some improvements could result from any period of rest in any different setting away from home. Nevertheless, marked and sustained improvements are made across the course of several admissions by the great majority of veterans. Reassurance can be given to new patients that they are likely to make significant progress if they engage and work hard at treatment. However, data available at present does not permit a precise assessment of improvements over time, although this will be possible in the future.

Longer-term outcome data is available from a follow-up study of Lee *et al.* (2005). A total of 80 individuals with PTSD from the Gulf War 1990/1991 were referred to eight specialist treatment units, including Combat Stress, where assessment and early management was performed by psychiatrists and therapists with an understanding of military service. Outcome was measured after 12 months through GP follow-up correspondence. A degree of successful outcome was found in 95 % of cases. This compares favourably with outcome data from other research. The authors conclude that treatments delivered by personnel with knowledge of military culture and combat reactions have a positive effect on the veteran's ability to engage in treatment and on their subsequent progress.

## FROM PRACTICE TO THEORY

The theoretical understanding of psychological reactions to traumatic events has swung from one extreme to another over the last 150 years. Early medical observations focused on physical symptoms seen after disasters and during wars, and the view prevailed that these symptoms were caused by organic pathology, even if such pathology could not be seen on clinical examination or at post-mortem. Diagnostic labels were awarded accordingly such as:

- railway spine;
- soldier's heart;
- disordered action of the heart;
- rheumatism;
- shell shock;
- effort syndrome;
- non-ulcer dyspepsia, and so on.

The development of psychoanalytical enquiry enriched diagnostic formulation during the First World War, so that certain behavioural disorders were understood in terms of psychological reactions. For example hysterical fugues, mutism, deafness, blindness, paralysis, odd gaits, or amnesia were conditions that were understood in terms of being involuntary or unconscious mental reactions to the horrors of war.

Whenever explanations exist that have the potential to relieve an individual from the demands of onerous duties, alternative views are always present. Hence 'railway spine' – the diagnosis given for symptoms seen after train collisions in England during the mid-Nineteenth century – became a derogatory term, especially after it was connected with fraudulent compensation claims. Given the necessity to keep as many men as possible at the front line during the First World War, the management of psychologically traumatised and exhausted men came under a number of pressures. One approach was to regard patients with nervous disorders as malingerers, or in a 'funk'. If this view were taken, a soldier would be returned to the front line. Another view was that 'neurasthenia' or 'shell shock' was a deliberate, conscious withdrawal from the horrors of war, and unacceptable, or even traitorous, under the circumstances. Disciplinary management was therefore used in some cases and could involve re-education (by diligent application to tasks the soldier disliked), shaming, or a court martial. Most commentators regard some of the 306 British and Commonwealth soldiers executed in the First World War for cowardice, desertion or insubordination to have been psychologically traumatised. Harsh attitudes were also found in general society, so that men sent back home with nervous disorders stood the risk of being regarded as cowards, disloyal, or constitutionally weak. Both they and their families could be subject to victimisation. Terms such as 'lack of moral fibre', 'malingerer' or 'neurotic' carried the implication that some form of shameful weakness, moral fault or cowardice played an important part in the development of psychological and behavioural problems seen in servicemen during wartime.

More sophisticated contributions to the understanding of traumatic reactions gradually emerged from a number of sources. These included:

- Lindemann (1944): Cocoanut Grove fire;
- Erickson (1976): Buffalo Creek dam burst;
- Raphael (1977): bereavement and disaster reactions;
- Dohrenwend (1981): Three Mile Island nuclear reactor accident;
- Sims *et al.* (1979): 'aftermath neurosis' following terrorist bombings;
- Shatan (1979): comparing reactions following the catastrophic stresses of natural disasters, man-made disasters, combat trauma, incarceration, Buffalo Creek, Hiroshima, and internment in the death camps;
- Ochberg (1996) added to the understanding of the complexity of stress reactions when he described the romantic attachment that

developed between a bank clerk and a hostage taker during a robbery in 1974 (the 'Stockholm Syndrome' or 'Hostage Identification Syndrome').

By 1980 the time was ripe for a new synthesis of ideas regarding trauma, or stress, reactions. This came with the publication of *Diagnostic and Statistical Manual of Mental Disorders III* (DSM III), and for the first time the inclusion of the diagnosis 'Post Traumatic Stress Disorder'.

One of the original intentions of the diagnosis of PTSD was to highlight the importance of the traumatic event itself as an aetiological factor in the development of complex fear-based disorders. A traumatic event could be considered as the sole sufficient cause of a psychological disorder. Predisposing factors might lower the threshold for the development of PTSD, but they were 'neither necessary nor sufficient to explain its occurrence' (ICD 10). Within the diagnostic classification the nature of the traumatising event had to be extreme, outside the range of normal human experience, and associated with profound levels of terror or helplessness. Thus, theoretically, any person, if they went through a certain type of event, would be so horrified and affected by it that they could be expected to suffer lasting psychological consequences.

This view facilitated an important shift in emphasis. Labels such as 'neurosis', or 'lack of moral fibre' could be abandoned, and replaced by an understanding of traumatic events – their quality, severity, intensity, duration and pathogenic potency. Importantly for sufferers, they could be relieved of feeling constitutionally inadequate because they had succumbed to the effects of a trauma. Holmes and Rahe attempted to quantify the degree of stress caused by different types of events, with a scale up to 100. With such a tool the potential existed for the estimation of thresholds for the onset of stress-related disorders. Treatments could thus become focused on the trauma reaction, rather than the individual's personal vulnerability or weakness.

However, this formulation of the relationship between traumatic events and psychological reactions has proved too simple. It is a fairly consistent finding that, after traumatic events, the majority of survivors do not suffer from PTSD or other chronic psychological reactions. Recent research shows that most sufferers of PTSD have not, in fact, suffered a traumatic event, but a more common sort of life event (Mol *et al.*, 2005). Furthermore, some individuals find that life is enhanced as a result of a life-threatening experience (see Table 5.7). It therefore remains necessary to continue to understand why some people are vulnerable to traumatic reactions and others are not.

**Table 5.7**   Reported benefits of traumatic experiences. Reproduced from Fletcher (1996), 'The Management of released hostages,' *Advances in Psychiatric Treatment*, 2, 232–40. Copyright, the British Journal of Psychiatry.

Closer relationships
Improved perspective on life
More emotional involvement
Conscious improvement
Cherished freedom
Stronger religious faith and enhanced personal values
Increased insight
Increased assertiveness
Enhanced self-esteem and self-understanding
Greater patience
Friendships born out of adversity
Improved understanding of other cultures

## RELATIONSHIP BETWEEN TRAUMA AND PSYCHOLOGICAL DISORDER

Current ideas about the relationship between traumatic events and PTSD can be briefly summarized in the following four ways:

(i) All individuals are susceptible to the development of PTSD. The likelihood of developing PTSD, and its severity, is proportional to the severity of the trauma (the dose–response curve, Figure 5.1);

(ii) There is an inverse relationship between the degree of personal vulnerability and the level of trauma or stress required to produce PTSD, i.e. the greater the degree of personal vulnerability the lower the level of trauma or stress required to produce PTSD (the stress–vulnerability diathesis). In vulnerable individuals, PTSD may be precipitated by 'life events' – such as divorce or death of a family member – that are not outside the range of normal events (Figure 5.2);

(iii) Only certain vulnerable individuals will develop PTSD after a traumatic event – others will not do so, irrespective of the severity of the trauma (Figure 5.3);

(iv) There are several factors to take into account. Individuals can develop trauma-related symptoms if exposed to traumatic events. Certain other vulnerable individuals will develop additional general psychopathology (e.g. anxiety and depression, substance misuse) in relation to stressful or traumatic events. Vulnerable individuals are likely to develop general psychopathologies and PTSD after a trauma, whereas resilient individuals will develop only PTSD (Figure 5.4).

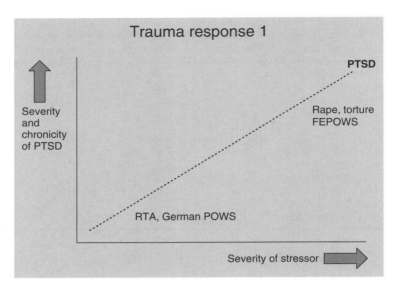

**Figure 5.1**  Trauma response 1

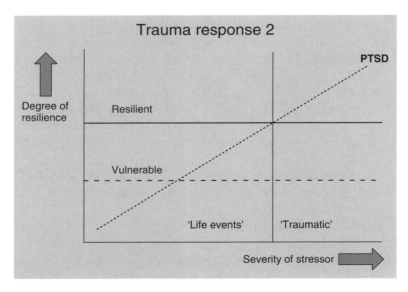

**Figure 5.2**  Trauma response 2

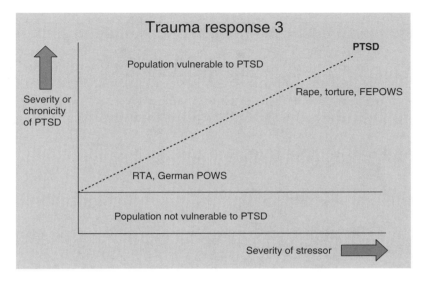

**Figure 5.3**   Trauma response 3

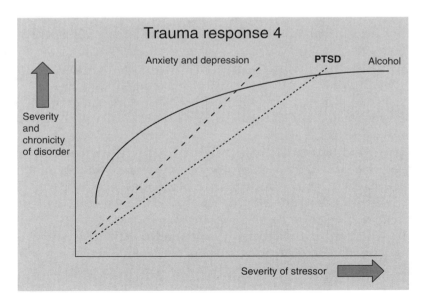

**Figure 5.4**   Trauma response 4

## From Theory to Practice

Veterans attending Combat Stress provide clinical examples of all of the above theoretical models. However, in practice the complexity of cases rarely permits a precise formulation of the way predisposing, precipitating and maintaining factors contribute to an individual's mental health problems. A number of histories will be given below as a means of demonstrating the complex links that exist between various types of trauma, pre-existing vulnerabilities, and the variety of associated psychological and social pathologies.

### Case 1: Graded moderate, simple

Mrs A is a 52-year-old lady living in Northern Ireland. She had a secure and happy family background, and presently enjoys a stable marriage and good relationships with her children. She walks with the aid of a stick.

During service in Northern Ireland she was aware of being followed by a car. She heard someone getting out of the vehicle and calling her name. As she turned she was shot. The bullet passed through her back causing spinal damage, grazed her heart, passed through the right upper lobe of her liver and exited through her flank. She was knocked off her feet and remembers her head banging on the tarmac of the road. The terrorist came and stood over her and pointed the gun directly at her. Mrs A pleaded for mercy. Either the gunman's weapon jammed or he changed his mind about shooting her. She heard the engine of the car revving loudly and the gunman left her. He was later caught and imprisoned for 14 years.

Many years after the shooting, whilst Mrs A was sitting in a hospital outpatient department, she was seen by the gunman who, in an intimidating manner, came and sat next to her. She was terrified and fled. Shortly afterwards she developed depression, attempted to take her life and required in-patient psychiatric care.

Mrs A currently has nightmares, cannot tolerate the sound of revving engines, suffers from irritability and poor concentration and is distressed if she talks about her experience. At the time of assessment she was concerned about the recent discovery of a breast lump and was awaiting a surgical appointment. She receives treatment for angina and osteoarthritis, and is prescribed two antidepressants by her general practitioner. Mrs A receives an 80% war pension for bullet wounds.

## Case 2: Graded severe, simple

Mr B is a 44-year-old single man. When he was 11 years old his mother committed suicide during the break-up of her marriage and he was brought up by his grandmother. During his army service in Belize, Mr B recovered body parts from an aircraft accident. Whilst serving in Northern Ireland he was subjected to 'brickings' and 'bottlings'. He saw the aftermath of a knee-capping incident. His most distressing experience was discovering the body of a young woman. Her legs had been tied behind her back so that they seemed 'folded in the wrong direction'. She had been shot through one of her buttocks and the bullet had exited through her breast.

For a period after discovering the body Mr B developed an alcohol problem but managed to overcome this without treatment. He 'tried and failed' to use cannabis to calm himself down. At the time of assessment his sleep was poor and he suffered from nightmares several times each week. Mr B could not watch television news for fear of being reminded about Northern Ireland and could not look at young females without thinking of the body of the young Irish woman. He tried to push any upsetting thoughts out of his mind and did not want talk to people who asked him about his army career.

What troubled Mr B most was his extreme level of aggression. His anger levels were so high that he feared going out and mixing with the public. He had frightened many people by displays of rage over minor incidents such as collisions between shopping trolleys. He stayed indoors during the daytime and used 24-hour supermarkets in the early hours of the morning to stock up on food. Mr B would not contemplate forming any close relationship because he thought it unfair to inflict his aggression on a partner.

During the assessment he was distracted and agitated. He also reported being distressed, frightened and exhausted by his unremitting state. He was not taking any medication, and was not in receipt of a war pension.

## Case 3: Graded moderate, complex

Mr C is 71-year-old man, married to his fourth wife. During childhood he was physically abused by his mother and was placed in care for a 9-month period. The family environment was characterized by violence and conflict. During his military service he was an ambulance driver and has vivid memories of attending a casualty who had been shot through the neck. He remembers blood spurting from the wound. He has other memories of undressing three bodies that, between them, had 48 gunshot wounds. On another occasion he collected the body parts of a baby who had been blown up in an explosion.

Mr C has typical features of PTSD, with nightmares, flashbacks, an inability to watch war films or medical programmes on television; he avoids talking about his experiences, and has a short temper, poor sleep and poor concentration. He has suffered from anxiety and depression and on seven occasions has attempted to take his life.

Mr C receives the support of a local community mental health team and a consultant psychiatrist. For a four-year period in the past, Mr C drank a bottle of spirits and a bottle of sherry per day, and suffered regular withdrawal symptoms. He recently had an operation for a prolapsed rectum. Mr C is prescribed an antidepressant and a beta–blocker. He receives a 30 % war pension for PTSD and hearing loss.


Case 4: Graded severe, complex

Mr D is a 48-year-old man who described his childhood and adolescence as 'terrible'. He came from a financially poor family, and communication between family members was full of conflict. He joined the Army and saw active service in Belfast and the Falkland Islands. He has never been able to talk about his experiences in Belfast.

His memories of fighting in the Falklands are so vivid that there are times when he thinks he is reliving them. His sleep is poor because he is troubled by nightmares and he screams at night. Mr D locks himself in his home because he has murderous thoughts about killing himself and taking other people with him. These thoughts scare him – he is frightened that he will act on them.

Mr D drinks a bottle of vodka per day and keeps a bottle of wine by the side of his bed. He says that alcohol reduces his suicidal and homicidal thoughts. In 1998 he attempted to take his life on two occasions and received in-patient hospital treatment. During one admission he absconded from hospital because he felt overwhelmed by thoughts of killing other people. He ran for 14 miles wearing only a pair of tracksuit bottoms.

In his view he has never settled into civilian life. His wife has left him and he has lost contact with his children. He has received five operations for carcinoma of the tonsil and has recently refused an offer of chemotherapy. He is prescribed an antidepressant, a hypnotic, and medication for hypertension and eczema. Mr D has received diagnoses of depression and PTSD. He receives a 70 % war pension for PTSD.

Case 5: Graded severe, complex

Mr E is a 32-year-old unemployed single man from a stable background who served in Northern Ireland and on exercise in various overseas locations. During a training run in Canada his friend collapsed and died in front of him, and he is very troubled by memories of his failure to save his friend's life. He has bad dreams of his Northern Ireland service, especially acts of hatred directed at British servicemen by the civilian population. In his dreams he sees stones being thrown, people spitting on him and hitting him. He wakes up in a cold sweat, panicking and struggling to breathe.

News items about Northern Ireland on television precipitate rages – he feels he will explode. During these rages he has hit people and smashed windows. He does everything he can to avoid reminders of his army service, but is frustrated, exasperated, tense and irritable because he is unable to achieve this. Mr E drinks beer, vodka and cider to blot out memories of Northern Ireland, and has on occasions suffered from severe alcohol withdrawal symptoms including visual hallucinations. At times he hears voices talking about him – one voice is evil, another is good. He thinks other people are talking about him and following him. He was diagnosed as suffering from schizophrenia 4 years ago, and receives treatment with a depot antipsychotic. Mr E receives a 70 % war pension for schizophrenia.

# THE FUTURE

The provision of charitable treatment services for veterans with mental health problems is sensitive to war pension arrangements. For instance, a recent proposal to offer lump sum compensation to psychologically traumatised veterans could have a considerable impact. This proposal recognises that there is little or no incentive for a veteran with a pension to seek treatment – indeed, making clinical progress could lead to the pension being reduced or withdrawn altogether. However, it cannot be assumed that individuals compensated with a lump sum would choose to spend their money on treatment. Given the poor problem-solving skills of some affected veterans and high levels of substance misuse, there is potential for any compensation payment to be used inappropriately or even to contribute to an exacerbation of problems.

Increasing pressures are being placed upon charitable agencies such as Combat Stress to focus exclusively on managing psychological trauma attributable to military service. Individuals with mental health problems that are not attributable to military service would be wholly cared for within the NHS. Given that the most severely affected veterans have difficulty engaging with NHS treatment services, this development may result in a neglect of serious psychopathology.

Current concepts underlying trauma-induced psychological disorder are due for an overhaul. The pendulum has swung from an over-emphasis on individual vulnerability (psychoneurosis) to an over-emphasis on the precipitating trauma (PTSD). A broader and more sophisticated understanding of the complex interactions between vulnerabilities and traumatic events is required. So, too, are research approaches that take an alternative view to the current mind–body split, and recognise the inextricable link between psychological and biological reactions to traumatic experiences.


## FINAL COMMENTS

This chapter has been written by a clinician, not a researcher. The views expressed have been formed as a result of listening to the histories of many hundreds of veterans. These veterans are among the most severely affected and therefore the opinions expressed will be subject to some sample bias, as well as personal bias. However, what seems indisputable is that war changes people. Some individuals benefit from their wartime experience; others simply cope with it and move on. For some veterans life will never be the same – there is a new understanding of what humans can do to each other, and of what they themselves could be capable of in certain circumstances. The world seems like a more unpredictable, dangerous and ugly place. It takes no great leap of imagination to consider that these veterans may never feel 'well' again. Clinics at Combat Stress show just how unwell veterans can be. Daily life is a struggle, and is compounded by physical illness, mental disorder, addiction, and social disadvantage.

It is a normal response for people to search for the meaning, or the cause, of changes in the way they experience life. Professors Lee and Jones have demonstrated with great clarity in their contributions that the 'Gulf War Syndrome' is a false explanation. It raises false hopes of treatment, of cure and perhaps of compensation. It compounds the difficulties veterans face. Those who bang this particular drum in the belief that they are helping veterans are mistaken. The media, when they report ill-substantiated health scares, add to the bewilderment, fears and hardships faced by the most vulnerable veterans.

Military personnel will always suffer in war. Many will give up their lives, others their limbs, and others their minds – and this sacrifice is expected. The imperative is to provide the wounded with the most appropriate care and treatment. The future of mental health treatment provision for ex-servicemen and women would best be served by carefully planned approaches between specialist charities such as Combat Stress, the NHS and the Veterans Agency. Combat Stress, with its expertise and almost 90 years of experience, has an invaluable role to play in training and supporting other NHS services, and treating the most severely affected.

## Acknowledgements

I am indebted to the following people for their assistance: Major (ret'd) Mike Burrows, Lt Col. (ret'd) Peter Poole, and Major (ret'd) Malcolm Belwood supplied information about Combat Stress welfare officers; Morag Heggie and Frances Robertson facilitated the collection of data on in-patients at Audley Court and Hollybush House; Elizabeth Stone assisted in collecting and compiling clinical data on in-patients at Audley Court and Hollybush House.

# REFERENCES

Dohrenwend, B., Dohrenwend, B. S., Warheit, G., Bartlett, G., Goldsteen, R., Goldsteen, K. and Martin, J. (1981). Stress in the community: a report to the President's Commission on the Accident at Three Mile Island, *Annals of the New York Academy of Sciences*, **365**, 159–174

Erikson, K. (1976). Loss of communality at Buffalo Creek, *American Journal of Psychiatry*, **133**, 302–4.

Fletcher, K. (1996). The management of released hostages, *Advances in Psychiatric Treatment*, **2**, 232–40.

Holmes, T. and Rahe, R. (1967). The Social Readjustment Rating Scale, *Journal of Psychosomatic Research*, **11**(2), 213–18.

Lee, H. A., Gabriel, R. and Bale, A. J. (2005). Clinical outcomes of Gulf Veterans' Medical Assessment Programme (GVMAP) referrals for Gulf Veterans with post traumatic stress disorder to specialised centres, *Military Medicine*, **170**, 400–406.

Lindemann, E. (1944). Symptomatology and management of acute grief, *American Journal of Psychiatry*, **101**, 141–48.

Mol, S., Arntz, J., Metsemakers, J., Dinant G.-J., Vilters-van Montford, P. and Knottnerus, A. (2005). Symptoms of post-traumatic events: evidence from an open population study, *British Journal of Psychiatry*, **186**, 494–99.

Ochberg, F. (1996) A primer on covering victims. *The Neiman Report* L(3), 21–26.

Raphael, B. (1977). Bereavement and prevention, *New Doctor*, **4**, 41–45.

Shatan, C., Haley, S. and Smith, J. (1979) Johnny comes marching home: The emotional context of combat stress. Concepts for the new Diagnostic and Statistical Manual (DSM–III) of Mental Disorders. Unpublished paper, based on a panel 'Can time heal all wounds: Diagnosis and Management of post-combat stress', presented at the annual meeting of the American Psychiatric Association, Toronto, May, 1977.

Sims, A., White, A. and Murphy, T. (1979). Aftermath neurosis: psychological sequalae of the Birmingham bombings in victims not seriously injured, *Medicine, Science and the Law*, **19** (2), 78–81.

SSAFA–Forces Help website: www.ssafa.org.uk/housing.html

# 6

# Clinical Outcomes

Harry Lee

## INTRODUCTION

A large cohort of Gulf War veterans has been studied as a result of
clinical examinations, interviews and investigations. These include the
US Comprehensive Clinical Evaluation Programme (CCEP) (Joseph,
1997), Combined analysis of the VA and DoD Gulf War Clinical Evaluation Programs (2002), the UK Gulf Veterans' Medical Assessment
Programme (Lee *et al.*, 2002; Lee *et al.*, 2005; Bale and Lee, 2005),
the Salamon report in France (2004) and the Australian Government
Department of Veterans Affairs (Forbes *et al.*, 2004; Kelsall *et al.*, 2004)
and Canadian Persian Gulf Cohort Study (2005). None of these has
revealed any unusual pattern of diseases amongst veterans or indeed any
unusual diseases. These studies, supported by others that investigated
mortality rates (Kang and Bullman, 1996; Macfarlane *et al.*, 2000;
DASA, 2005, 2006), have not shown excess mortality rates or particular prevalence of any single disease or system disorder. The substantive
report on the health of Gulf veterans by the IOM (Rosof and Hernandez,
2001) made no references to 'Gulf War Syndrome', though it did identify
recognised disorders such as irritable bowel syndrome and chronic
fatigue syndrome. These disorders are amenable to established treatment strategies, albeit not always successful, as emphasised in that
report.

*War and Health: Lessons from the Gulf War*   Edited by Harry Lee & Edgar Jones
© 2007 John Wiley & Sons, Ltd

# NEUROLOGY

A large amount of clinical and research work has been undertaken as a result of suggestions made by Haley et al. (1997a) that a number of Gulf War syndromes exist. This group thought they had made a case definition, but this is highly debatable and has not been replicated. Furthermore, they could not define a cause and effect relationship such as, for example, exists between tobacco consumption and lung cancer, or risk factors associated with age. Haley's original study was based on 606 personnel drawn from US 24 Reserve Naval Mobile Construction Battalion, who were asked to complete self-report questionnaires. There were 249 responses (41 % response rate) and 175 reported health problems, including 160 veterans who had sought medical advice. Then, as a result of factor analysis, symptom patterns were identified in 63 veterans that fell into six separate groups, which Haley termed 'syndromes'. There were three major syndromes: impaired cognition (12 veterans), confusion ataxia syndrome (21) and arthromyoneuropathy (22). The first and third syndromes were designated primary, for they had few so-called overlapping features. It must be emphasised that the data on which these syndromes were based on questionnaires, not clinical examination. Furthermore, as pointed out by Landragran (1997), observations were based on a small sample size, which comprised less than 4 % of the unit under investigation and well below 1 % of those deployed by America to the Gulf. Ferrari and Russell (2001) also considered the research to be flawed on the basis of low response rate, concentration on a single reserve unit (the experiences of which may not have been representative of the whole deployed force, this group being a reserve unit), and reliance on self-reported illnesses and exposures. They heavily criticised the lack of a control cohort, which was particularly damaging to any interpretation of this study. Subsequent larger, well-designed studies failed to replicate Haley's findings (Unwin et al., 1999), as supported by comments of Murphy (1999) and Ismail et al. (1999).

Haley et al. (1997b, c) then evaluated neurological function in Gulf War veterans based on the original small groups referred to above. This involved studying 23 cases from study 1 compared with 20 controls, but the 23 were made up of the five worst affected by syndrome 1, 13 worst affected by syndrome 2 and the five worst affected by syndrome 3. The control group comprised 10 veterans from the same unit who reported no ill health in study 1, and 10 members of the unit who did deploy to the Gulf. A panel of six neurologists who were blinded as to their case status, reviewed the findings in all subjects and tried to make a diagnosis, but they could not find statistically or clinically significant differences between cases or controls with regard to neurological examination, blood tests, magnetic resonance imaging (MRI) and single photon emission computer tomography (SPECT) brain scans. The panel concluded that the clinical and laboratory findings were nonspecific and not sufficient to diagnose any known syndrome in any subgroup of subjects.

Next, Haley *et al.* (2000a) reported specifically on their findings using proton magnetic resonance spectroscopy, as an alternative to imaging methods MRI and SPECT. The aim of this study was to explore brain biochemistry in individuals and concentrated on N-acetyl aspartate (NAA) in small areas of the brain and measuring NAA/CR (creatine) and CHO/CR (choline/creatine ratios) in three distinct areas of the brain, the pons, and the left and right basal ganglia. These were chosen because it is well known that basal ganglia are affected in Parkinson's' disease, Huntington's chorea, some affective disorders and some dementias. However, these observations were made in a small selected clinical sample of unusually old and ill veterans, with an equally small control group. The study showed, taking all three brain areas together, that there was no significant difference in NAA/CR ratios between cases and controls. For the basal ganglia, there was a pattern of significant reduction of NAA/CR ratio in syndrome 2, but not for syndromes 1 and 3. In the pons, NAA/CR ratio between case controls was not significantly different and even Haley admitted that the parameters used in their study were very sensitive and non-specific indicators of loss of neuronal tissue. This group (Haley *et al.*, 2000b) then reported on the correlation between plasma homovanillic acid and proton MR spectroscopy, and central dopamine activity and basal ganglia injury. Again all investigations were done on small numbers of veterans. A larger study is now under way in the US to see if such findings can be replicated. Meanwhile, in the UK, based on advice given by the Medical Research Council, the MoD has decided it will not proceed with further neuroimaging studies (Hansard, 2005).

As a result of these limited studies, Haley (2000) made the astonishing claim that 'there appears to be a serious epidemic of neurodegenerative disease from toxic chemical exposures in Gulf War veterans . . . ' Such unjustified speculation was roundly condemned by Doebbeling *et al.* (2000) on the basis of Haley's poor methodology and the failure to replicate his findings in other reports based on large population studies. His findings did not provide support for the hypothesis of a 'Gulf War

Syndrome' and it should be emphasised that he did not include a real control group.

Ismail *et al.* (1999) failed to find any evidence of a 'Gulf War Syndrome', let alone a number of other specific syndromes. Furthermore, Haley's studies comprised a snapshot of findings in particular veterans at a particular time, which could not indicate whether findings would improve, deteriorate or remain static had they been done earlier or a few years later.

Menon *et al.* (2004) reported on their findings about the pathogenesis of 'Gulf War Syndrome'. They postulated that because the hippocampal region is highly vascularised, it might be more vulnerable to toxic substances in the circulation. They used *in vivo* proton MR spectroscopy (MRS) to study the left and right hippocampi of consenting Gulf War veterans ($n = 15$), of whom 10 purportedly had 'Gulf War Syndrome' and five did not, and a control group of Vietnam veterans ($n = 6$). They too looked at NAA/creatine ratios, but found no laterality differences between the three groups. They found that the NAA/creatine ratio of the younger group (only Gulf veterans) was significantly lower than that of the older group, leading to the hypothesis that the lower NAA/creatine ratio for the 'Gulf War Syndrome' group pointed to the existence of hippocampal dysfunction. Again, this study was flawed by the very small numbers investigated, particularly as it appears that six of the ten who purported to have 'Gulf War Syndrome' did not suffer from any Gulf related illness. In addition, they chose Vietnam veterans, who would have been significantly older, as a control group.

David *et al.* (2002) studied cognitive (functional) disturbances of mood in UK veterans of Op Granby. They found that disturbances of mood are more prominent than quantifiable cognitive defects in Gulf War veterans and probably lead to subjective underestimated validity. They also noted that task performance deficits can themselves be explained to some degree by depressed mood. However, this study relied on self-reported information, on questionnaires, and they admitted the problem of recall and reporting biases, as observed by Southwick *et al.* (1997).Southwick *et al.* emphasised that the major limitation of their study was reliance on self-reported questionnaires, and that such reports are less valid and less reliable than clinical assessments. Furthermore, those who were sent questionnaires had previously been invited to participate in a previous study. Nonetheless, this group suggested that their findings were probably related to active deployment and not necessarily to specific Gulf related exposures.

Storzbach *et al.* (2001) studied a group of patients associated with Persian Gulf service with persistent symptoms, but with no medical explanation, such as fatigue, muscle pain, memory deficits, beginning during or after the war. There were 239 cases with unexplained symptoms and a control group of 112 without symptoms. They found that the majority of cases with neurobehavioural symptoms had no objective evidence of neurobehavioural deficit. They also made the important observation that some with symptoms might have been from the unhealthy end of the Gulf War veteran population prior to the war.

In another well designed study on 176 Persian Gulf veterans with neurological symptoms (Rivera-Zayas *et al.*, 2001), who investigated both motor and sensory neurological parameters, although recognising some limitations of their study, they found no evidence of a definite generalised neuropathic pattern in Gulf War veterans. Likewise, Newmark and Clayton (1995) did not find any evidence of peripheral neuropathy in their study.

In a small but meticulous study, Amato *et al.* (1997) studied 20 Gulf veterans with severe muscle fatigue, weakness or myalgia that interfered with their daily activities. Investigations included single-fibre electromyography, nerve conduction studies, muscle biopsies, exercise forearm tests and various blood tests. They concluded that, despite severe subjective symptoms, the majority of their patients did not have objective evidence of neuromuscular diseases nor were potential exposures to toxins during the Persian Gulf War likely to be responsible for their patients' symptoms. It is perhaps not surprising, given the high incidence of neurocognitive, neurobehavioural, affective and peripheral neurological symptoms, that so much research has been directed towards investigating whether there is a common central nervous system or peripheral nervous system neuropathic aetiology to veterans' ill health.

In a large study by Joseph *et al.* (1997), of 20 000 veterans evaluated, peripheral neuropathy was diagnosed in 42 (0.2 %). Likewise, Lee *et al.* (2005) did not observe any unusual neurological results in a group of Gulf veterans attending GVMAP with neurological symptoms. Furthermore, Bale and Lee (2005), in a large observational study, did not discover any unexpected neurological disorders. In fact, amongst 3233 Gulf veterans, they found only one case of peripheral neuropathy and that was alcohol related. In the Australian study (Kelsall *et al.*, 2004), no reference was made to any neurological disorder.

In a very extensive, well-referenced review of peripheral neuropathy, England and Asprey (2004) made no mention of any connection between any form of peripheral neuropathy and deployment to the Gulf 1990–91.

Cherry *et al.* (2001) found, on the basis of self-report questionnaires and the use of a mannequin diagram, that there was increased peripheral nerve damage in veterans. Although they proposed a possible linkage to organophosphate exposure, none of the veterans were investigated clinically. Their endeavours to provide evidence of peripheral neuropathy were based on pain distribution on mannequins, which suggested a dose response relationship between the number of inoculations allegedly received and the peripheral neurological factor. They also found a dose response rate between the declared number of days of handling pesticides, exposure to oil well fires, using protective nerve agents (i.e. pyridostigmine bromide – NAPS) and using insect repellent with various factors. However, a carefully controlled and thorough study by Sharief *et al.* (2002), on neurophysiological evaluation of neuromuscular symptoms in Gulf War veterans, concluded that Gulf War related neuromuscular symptoms are not associated with specific impairments of peripheral nerves, the neuromuscular junction or skeletal muscles. Their results argued against any potential toxic causes for neuromuscular symptoms experienced by Gulf War veterans. Joseph *et al.* (2004), using electrodiagnostic investigations in Gulf War veterans in a controlled study, found evidence of a decreased incidence of peripheral neuropathy in Gulf War veterans. In a meticulous study, Davis *et al.* (2004) undertook clinical and laboratory assessment of distal peripheral nerves in Gulf War veterans and their spouses. This research used the time honoured approach of careful clinical examination and nerve conduction studies, and was the largest controlled objective evaluation of neurologic health of Gulf War veterans comparing deployed and non-deployed veterans and their spouses. Importantly, they noted that deployed veterans potentially exposed to neurotoxins from the Khamisayah ammunition dump depot explosion did not significantly differ in distal symmetric polyneuropathy (DSP) prevalence compared to non-exposed DV. Their overall conclusion was that neither veterans deployed during the Gulf War nor their spouses had a higher prevalence of DSP compared with non-deployed veterans (era group) and spouses, very similar findings to Sharief *et al.* (2002).

There is a number of reports about the health consequences of Australian veterans who served in the Gulf (Op Granby 1990–91). Firstly, Forbes *et al.* (2004) revisited the issue of factor analysis of self-reported symptoms, the basis for Gulf War Syndrome first proposed by Haley *et al.* (1997a), but critically disputed by Unwin *et al.* (1999).

They compared 1322 male Gulf War veterans with a control group of 1459. They concluded that symptoms complained of did not show a unique pattern of self-reported symptoms amongst these veterans, and emphasised the well documented evidence of increased self-reporting of symptoms amongst Gulf War veterans. Later, this group (Kelsall *et al.* 2005) reported their clinical findings in a cross-sectional study on 1424 male Australian Gulf War veterans who completed a postal questionnaire, of whom 1382 went on to participate in a complete neurological examination, compared to a randomly selected military comparison group. They concluded that Gulf War veterans reported more neurological-type symptoms but did not show any evidence of increased neurological defects based on objective physical signs.

Haley (2003) observed there was a greater incidence of amyotrophic lateral sclerosis (ALS), also known as motor neurone disease or Lou–Gehrig syndrome, in young Gulf War veterans than expected, suggesting a war related environmental trigger. Unsubstantiated media reports in the UK in 2003 and 2004 also suggested a link between Gulf War service and motor neurone disease (MND). Studies by Horner *et al.* (2003) also suggested that MND was more likely to be associated with Gulf War service. However, the robust research of Weisskopf *et al.* (2005) showed that there was only a marginally increased risk of MND with military service, but not restricted specifically to Gulf War service. This non-statistically significant increase appeared to be largely independent of the branch of military service, the time period served or in which conflict served. In their review of ALS and military service, Beghi and Morrison (2005) concluded there would be little to gain about understanding ALS causation by further large studies of the US Gulf War veteran population.

In an interesting investigation, Carson *et al.* (2003) studied the outcome of patients with medically unexplained symptoms who attended a neurology outpatient clinic. This was a prospective cohort study. Of the 300 original attendees, 90 were further investigated and symptoms were rated 'not at all' or 'somewhat' to explainable organic disease. However, further studies did not reveal a single case of an organic cause for the presenting complaint. Over half the patients presented to neurologists with symptoms that were rated as largely or completely medically unexplained and had not improved 8 months later. In no case was there a disease explanation for the original presenting symptom.

Jones and Wessely (2005) reviewed the issue of 'Hearts, guts, minds, somatisation in the military from 1900'. They concluded that somatoform disorders did not disappear from the military in a smooth progression as society's understanding of psychological issues advanced. Rather, there was a change in physical focus from heart to gut as new medical priorities arose, and I would suggest subsequently to the locomotor system and the nervous system.

Vasterling and Bremner (2006), in their review of neuropsychological and neuro-imaging research, emphasise the inherent and, for most part, unavoidable methodological problems with such investigations. They noted the paucity of objective exposure data in veterans, virtually no baseline data and, most importantly, the significant time lapse between Gulf War deployment and subsequent use of objective neuropsychological and brain imaging techniques. The time-lapse factor itself introduces many more confounding factors in any studies undertaken. Further, they raise the important issue about the possibility that pre-existing health vulnerability factors may have influenced subsequent health outcomes of Gulf veterans.

When reviewing four large population based epidemiological studies comparing neurological examination as well as some neurophysiological investigations, no differences were found between Gulf War veterans and military or civilian controls (Rose and Brix, 2006). Very tellingly, in their analysis of neurological studies, they concluded 'that if a neurological examination in a Gulf War veteran is within normal limits, then extensive neurological testing is unlikely to diagnose occult neurological disorders'.

In conclusion, there are no robust studies that provide convincing evidence of either central nervous system or peripheral nervous system specific damage as a result of service in the Gulf.

Clearly, it is reasonable for a veteran and his attendant physician to question whether any specific neurological problem is related to Gulf War service. However, from the GVMAP database, we have not seen the emergence of any unusual pattern of neurological disease or unusual neurological disorders. Examples of neurological disease have been seen (Bale and Lee, 2005), but not beyond what would be expected. For example, Bale and Lee found 15 cases of multiple sclerosis all having been diagnosed prior to attendance at MAP, they were all male (but 90 % of forces deployed to the Gulf were male). Although that study could not pronounce on a prevalence rate, it should be noted that morbidity statistics from general practice for men provide estimates of 2 per 10 000 for the incidence rate in the age group 25–44, 6 per 10 000 for the prevalence and 20 per 10 000 for GP consultation. One case of MND has been seen at GVMAP, he being in the younger age cohort.

However, Leigh (2002, personal communication) indicated that 20 % of his patients had an onset below the age of 45, although admittedly this was probably skewed because of the known interest of his unit. Most cases appear between the ages of 50 and 60, with a median at 62. Prevalence varies widely, except in North America and Europe where it is 4–5 per 100 000, with an incidence of 1–2 per 100 000. There is no known cause for MND and those cases occurring in veterans who served in the Gulf could happen by chance.

In an interesting and comprehensive review (Binder and Campbell, 2004), the subjects of medically unexplained symptoms, including pseudo neurological illness, silicone breast implant illness, fibromyalgia, chronic fatigue syndrome, multiple chemical sensitivities, toxic mould related illness, sick building syndrome, Persian-Gulf related illnesses, psychological stress and disease were covered. They noted considerable overlap between Gulf War illnesses and medically unexplained symptoms. The evidence obtained strongly suggested that some of these illnesses may well be associated with objective cognitive abnormalities rather than traditionally defined neurological disease. They proposed that cognitive abnormalities might be caused by a complex interaction between biological and psychological factors. They made the important observation that a considerable number of diagnostic problems are accentuated by the fact that often patients (veterans) are poor historians. Many patients may admit to histories of severe stressors and psychiatric problems, but an inability to talk about stressors increases the likelihood of suffering from physiological forms of stress.

It is reasonable to suggest, in view of the foregoing, that further large-scale epidemiological neurological studies into Gulf War illness, searching for a link between potential Gulf War exposures and neurological disease, be suspended. Better to concentrate on management programmes for the veterans' existing health problems.

## OTHER MEDICAL CONDITIONS

Apart from neuro-behavioural (affective), cognitive disorders and neurological conditions, no other human system has attracted so much research attention. Perhaps, therefore, it is not surprising that studies have not shown the incidence and/or prevalence of unusual diseases or an unusual pattern of diseases amongst veterans. Studies such as Lee *et al.* (2005) and Bale and Lee (2005) have shown neither any untoward results of investigations nor the emergence of any unexpected diseases, on the basis of ICD-10 classifications (WHO, 1992). Furthermore, controlled studies, including Unwin *et al.* (1999) and Eisen *et al.* (2005), have found only a few chronic physical health conditions that seem to be associated with 1991 Gulf War deployment. Nevertheless, it has to be acknowledged that much of this assessment has been based on both self-reported health status and self-reported exposures. Interestingly, Eisen *et al.* (2005), who compared a deployed and non-deployed group of veterans 10 years after the Gulf War, found that physical health was similar.

## RENAL DISEASE

Eisen *et al.* (2005), using a similar investigatory approach to GVMAP (Lee *et al.*, 2005), found no difference in blood urea nitrogen concentration, serum magnesium concentration, prevalence of proteinuria and leucocytes on urine examination, very similar to the observations of Lee *et al.* (2005). Their studies found no increased incidence or prevalence of any unusual renal disease, which again is confirmed by the Salamon report (2004).

There are no reports indicating an increased incidence of any type of renal disease amongst Gulf War veterans (Joseph, 1997; Lee *et al.*, 2005; Bale and Lee, 2005; Salamon, 2004; Eisen *et al.*, 2005). Bale and Lee (2005) reported two cases of bladder detrusor muscle dysfunction as a result of having taken NAPS (pyridostigmine bromide). The 3233 patients who attended GVMAP were divided into three cohorts of 1000. The incidence of renal disease amongst the first, second and third cohorts was 1.3, 1.4 and 1.5 % respectively. When compared with national statistics, there was no evidence of any increased rate of end-stage renal failure amongst Gulf War veterans using an age-adjusted approach. The incidence of end-stage renal failure in 1990–91 was 80–120 per million patients. However, a recent report (Clase *et al.*, 2004) suggested that at least 404 per million population in Europe had end-stage renal failure. On this basis, therefore, we might have expected to see 2.4 patients with end stage renal failure attending MAP, when in fact we only saw one.

Similarly, Joseph (1997) found only 12 (0.06 %) cases of renal insufficiency in a cohort of 20 000 Gulf War veterans, and glomerulonephritis in another 13 (0.07 %). Bale and Lee (2005) found 22 cases (1 %) of nephrolithiasis and 15 cases of glomerulonephritis, none of which could be attributed to service in the Gulf. In the French series (Salamon, 2004), there was a slight excess of cases with nephrolithiasis, but this probably reflects the fact that French military personnel are often deployed to hot, arid regions of Africa. It is virtually impossible to develop renal stones as a result of a 6-month deployment to a hot area.

## RESPIRATORY DISORDERS

Of Gulf related organic diseases, the most common were of a respiratory nature, amongst which asthma was the most frequent (Bale and Lee, 2005), while there were also 17 cases of sinusitis and 14 of rhinitis, two of which were Gulf related. Nasal sinus problems were noted in 10 % of Australian Gulf War veterans compared with an incidence of 7 % in a control group (Kelsall *et al.*, 2004). Elsewhere, Karlinsky *et al.* (2004) investigated the issue of increased prevalence of self-reported respiratory symptoms among Servicemen deployed during the 1990–91 Gulf War. They studied 1036 deployed and 1103 non-deployed veterans of the Gulf War. This was a comprehensive evaluation based on medical history and pulmonary function tests, as a result of which they concluded: 'our findings did not confirm the hypothesis that deployment to the Gulf War in 1990–91 resulted in an increased prevalence of clinically significant pulmonary abnormalities 10 years later'.

It has been observed that Danish veterans of the Gulf War have a high incidence of self-reported dyspnoea (Svensson *et al.*, 2000). They compared 686 Gulf veterans with 231 controls. All underwent stringent clinical examinations and investigations. They found that the high prevalence of dyspnoea amongst Gulf War veterans could be largely attributed to their high prevalence of mental and cognitive symptoms, suggesting psychogenic dyspnoea. In this same report, they admitted that, in spite of 'extraordinary recruitment efforts, only 53 % of eligible deployed and 39 % of eligible non-deployed veterans participated'. They also conceded that their study's cross-sectional design precluded making cause and effect conclusions. In addition they did not collect data blindly, which might have introduced observer bias.

## PHYSICAL FUNCTION STATUS (SP36)

In a very sensible and balanced review of the Eisen *et al.* (2005) article by Komatroff (2005), he emphasised that the paper reported on a self-selected and self-reported basis. From a number of observational and epidemiological studies, Komatroff concluded that armed forces personnel deployed to the Persian Gulf region were statistically significantly more likely to report chronic debilitating symptoms than were personnel deployed to other areas. Those studies that defined functional status (Kang *et al.*, 2000; Unwin *et al.*, 1999) found no or very little difference between evaluated functional status and employment between deployed and non-deployed groups. What Kang *et al.* found was that Gulf veterans seem to require more clinic and hospital visits than an era group. This was supported by Eisen *et al.* (2005), who found that there was a clinically insignificant decrease in the SP36 (physical and functional assessment) physical component seen amongst deployed veterans.

Whilst armed forces personnel deployed to the Gulf were more likely to report debilitating chronic symptoms and other problems, no differences were found in their subsequent rates of hospitalisation (Gray *et al.*, 1996) or mortality (Kang and Bullman, 1996; MacFarlane *et al.*, 2000; Defence Analytical Services Agency (DASA), 2005, 2006), or reproductive health (Cowan *et al.*, 1997; Araneta *et al.*, 2000).

Komatroff (2005) explains that exposures that could have been experienced by Gulf War veterans are based on murky evidence and remain controversial. Again, accurate records of each suspected exposure to various agents do not exist, and with the passage of time recall becomes ever more confused (Greenberg, 2004). Komatroff emphasised that although Eisen *et al.* (2005) found functional status to be worse amongst deployed participants, the change was statistically significant, but of a very small differential. He, like others (Lee *et al.*, 2002, 2005), did not find that the constellation of reported symptoms constituted a unique syndrome.

The concluding remarks of Komatroff (2005) are well worth re-emphasising. He referred in turn to two Institute of Medicine reports (Fulco *et al.*, 2000; Colwill, 2003) and emphasised the need to:

(i) establish reliably recorded immunisations given to military personnel;
(ii) closely monitor health of armed forces personnel during conflict, regardless of whether physical injuries have occurred.
(iii) finally, perform similar health assessments simultaneously on randomly chosen and matched personnel who had deployed to a non-combat zone.

Also, importantly, regularly monitor various exposures during combat.

# MUSCULOSKELETAL DISORDERS

Compston *et al.* (2002) reported a small study on 17 Gulf War litigants chosen for bone biopsy. In this report, no mention was made of a patient's nutritional status, if a patient was suffering from bowel disease, neither was anything reported about biochemical aspects of calcium/phosphate metabolism and bone alkaline phosphatase. No mention was made about the lifestyles of these 17 litigants. The control element of this study was from 13 previously healthy men investigated for another publication. Histories referred to '2 or 4 months in Gulf during the war and most spent time at Blackadder Camp, where there was obvious spraying by environmental health officers of organophosphates'. This was the nearest we get to any specific statement about exposure. Quite extraordinarily, the comment was made 'At least four exposed to sarin'. There is no evidence whatsoever that any Gulf War veteran was exposed to sarin. They say they could not find any accurate information about vaccination history, which is contrary to the publications from GVMAP (Lee *et al.*, 2002, 2005). They chose to record an alcohol excess above 10 units as being significant. They also stated: 'None of the men has osteoporosis'. No measurements of BMI were made. There were many assumptions made in this paper about comparing organophosphate exposure amongst Gulf War veterans and farmers involved with sheep dipping. We were not told if some of the litigants were in the agricultural industry. The authors agreed that the clinical relevance of their observed changes in bone formation is unclear. There was no evidence to support the media claims of 'brittle bone disease'.

The editorial by Freemont (2002) on the Compston *et al.* paper contained a number of inaccuracies such as 'Gulf War veterans suffer proportionately more hospitalisations for certain specific diagnoses', which was not supported by the thorough work of Gray *et al.* (1996). Freemont continues: '. . . this study is interesting because it raises the possibility of a specific disorder resulting from service in the Gulf War and this is backed up by hard data'. This is an unreasonable statement to make, as the 17 subjects in the study were self-reported and self-selected, and given the considerable heterogeneity of bone biopsy findings, these do not add up to hard data. Freemont makes the mistake of comparing Gulf veterans' exposures with repeated annual exposures by farm workers to organophosphates in the agricultural industry. Why pyridostigmine bromide or vaccinations were brought into the argument is difficult to fathom. The issue of mustard gas was also brought into the review, though no evidence exists to suggest that this agent was ever used. Both the paper and review were disappointing and based on flawed evidence. Blatchley, Lee and Bolton (2003) strongly criticised the design, numbers involved and conclusions reached on such a small self-selected group. Elsewhere (Bale and Lee, 2005) have only found evidence of bone disease that is clearly related to service physical stresses.

Bale and Lee (2005) found the most common musculoskeletal disorder seen amongst veterans was osteoarthritis in 117 (4 %), only five of which could be related to Gulf deployment as a result of trauma. Next, there were 32 examples (1 %) of mechanical low back pain, only one of which could be related to Gulf service. There were 26 cases of arthropathy/polyarthropathy, none of which could be related to Gulf service and likewise 23 cases of chondromalaciae patellae. Kelsall *et al.* (2004) found osteoarthritic disorders (23 %) were most commonly complained of in Australian Gulf War veterans, but no more so than in a control group.

In the clinical outcomes reported by Eisen *et al.* (2005), they refer to an increased risk for the development of fibromyalgia (fibrositis/fibromyalgia). Unfortunately, Eisen *et al.* suggest that chronic fatigue syndrome among Gulf War veterans may be a different disorder than the sporadically occurring syndrome in the United States. This seems to be a rather indecisive approach and an attempt to move the goal-posts. Although musculoskeletal disorders were the most frequently diag-nosed, no specific mention of fibromyalgia (F) was made by Kelsall *et al.* (2004). Smith *et al.* (2000), in a large analysis of Gulf veteran hospi-talisation data, found a very slight risk of post war hospitalisation for fibromyalgia, but thought the risk difference (compared to non-deployed veterans) was due to the Gulf War veterans' clinical evaluation program, which had started in 1994. They concluded there was no evidence to support Gulf War service and disease associations for those reviewed [systemic lupus erythematosus (SLE), amyotrophic lateral sclerosis (ALS) and (F)]. Bale and Lee (2005) had a very high threshold for diagnosing fibromyalgia and, perhaps not surprisingly, we did not see any cases to which this diagnosis could be applied. The very existence of fibromyalgia has been seriously questioned (Quiner and Coan, 1999). These authors preferred the concept of clinical mechanical allodynia as being the funda-mental underlying pathophysiological phenomenon. What this may be remains open to question. As Quiner and Coan stated, it seems to be that fibromyalgia is an entrenched diagnostic label – at least in rheumato-logical circles – but is a label so easily abused as to become meaning-less and again not amenable to specific treatment. One is mindful of the comments by Lewis (1944), when he wrote: 'Diagnosis is a system of more or less accurate guessing in which the end point achieved is a name. These names applied to disease come up to assume the importance of specific entities, whereas they are for the most part no more than insecure, and therefore temporary conceptions'. How well this fits the concept and the fate of 'Gulf War Syndrome' in medical and popular culture.

## SKIN DISORDERS

There have been claims about an unusual pattern of skin disorders amongst veterans that might contribute to their ill health. However, in the observational study by Bale and Lee (2005), 81 cases of dermatitis (eczema, dermatitis, skin allergies) were found, of which only five could be related to service in the Gulf. There were 47 cases of psoriasis (1 %), only two of which could be Gulf related, followed by urticaria/erythema in 25 cases (1 %), none of which were Gulf related, and acne 23 (1 %) of which two were Gulf related. There were 18 veterans with skin infections (1 %), none of which could be temporally related to Gulf service. Likewise, Hotopf *et al.* (2000) could not find any relationship between vaccinations and increased incidence of eczema or psoriasis problems. Higgins *et al.* (2002) undertook a study of 111 disabled, 98 non-disabled Gulf veterans and 133 disabled non-Gulf veterans. This study reported a twofold increase in seborrhoeic dermatitis, but the over-riding conclusion was that skin disease does not appear to contribute to ill health in Gulf War veterans. Seborrhoeic dermatitis is but a mild skin complaint. Kelsall *et al.* (2004) found a slight increase in skin conditions (other than dermatitis, psoriasis, eczema, skin cancer or malignant melanoma) in veterans, 14 % compared with 11 % in a control group. An excess of usual or unusual skin disorders has not featured in any other reports.

Eisen *et al.* (2005) concluded that the sample size of their study was not sufficient to detect any adverse health outcome from a specific exposure as experienced by some veterans, or a moderate increase in risk for rare diseases. Nevertheless, they noted that dermatological conditions such as psoriasis, which is known to worsen with stress, was not increased statistically among deployed veterans. They conclude, importantly, 10 years after the Gulf War (Op Granby 1990–91) that the physical health of veterans is similar to that of non-deployed veterans.

## GASTROINTESTINAL DISEASE

Although Gulf War veterans often report vague symptoms of gastrointestinal discomfort, there was nothing unusual found in the observational study by Bale and Lee (2005). Digestive system disorders were found in 154 veterans (out of 3254, i.e. 4.7 %), amongst which there were 34 (1 %) cases of irritable bowel syndrome (IBS) without concomitant psychiatric disorder. There were eight cases of IBS associated with Gulf service, but with no specific aetiology. Bale and Lee (2005) identified six cases of IBS, the onset of which coincided with taking NAPS (pyridostigmine bromide). There were six cases of Crohn's disease, all but one occurring in males and one having a family history. There has only been one report suggesting a possible increased risk of gall bladder disease amongst Gulf War veterans (Milner *et al.*, 1998). Subsequently Haley *et al.* (2004) reported on their study of autonomic nervous system function in 22 veterans from his original SEABEE cohort with chronic symptoms. They found blunted circadian variation in autonomic regulation of sinus node function in veterans with 'Gulf War Syndrome'. From this they extrapolated that subtle autonomic dysfunction might account for excessive and increasing rates of cholecystitis and cholecystenterostomies in veterans. However, an increased incidence of gall bladder disease has not been found in any of the large international clinical studies. Cholelithiasis was found in 11 veterans in whom the diagnosis was extant (Lee and Bale, 2005).

In the Australian study (Kelsall *et al.*, 2004), no differences were found in bowel disorders (diarrhoea, constipation, bleeding) between a Gulf War veterans group and a comparison group, there being a 10 % incidence in both. Likewise, in the French study (Salamon, 2004), no increased incidence or unusual pattern of bowel disorder was noted.

The important publication by the Institute of Medicine (USA) (2001) presented guidelines on treating symptoms and syndromes of Gulf War veterans. In their diagnostic list of disorders that they felt were amenable to treatment, they named chronic fatigue syndrome, depression, fibromyalgia, headache, irritable bowel syndrome, panic disorder and post-traumatic stress disorder. Nowhere in this volume was mention made of 'Gulf War Syndrome'.

# AUTOIMMUNE DISEASE AND IMMUNOLOGICAL DYSFUNCTION

On a number of occasions there have been reports of veterans claiming their 'immune systems have been knackered' and hence more prone to infections and autoimmune diseases. Only three cases of SLE were found by Bale and Lee (2005) amongst 3233 veterans reviewed. Also, they did not find any unusual pattern of results in those patients where serum electrophoresis had been carried out or serum immunoglobulins measured (Lee *et al.*, 2005). In all other large international investigations, autoimmune diseases have not featured as a particular problem.

Recently Peakman *et al.* (2006) undertook a detailed analysis of studies investigating any link between vaccinations received by Gulf veterans and subsequent immunological dysfunction. Many of the studies were undertaken as a result of the speculation by Rook and Zumla (1997), that there might be a shift in immune response from a Th1 to a Th2 pattern. Peakman *et al.* (2006) found little evidence of such an effect. They only found a weak relationship, and this subject to recall bias as also observed by Greenberg *et al.* (2003), for any epidemiological evidence of a link between multiple vaccines and multi-symptom illness, which has little to do with any claimed adverse effect on the immune system.

# REPRODUCTIVE OUTCOMES

Following speculative and anecdotal media reports in the early 1990s (Tipit, 1994; Briggs, 1995; Jerome *et al.*, 1995), it was suggested that there were problems with the reproductive health of Gulf War veterans. There were popular press allegations that because of potential toxic exposures during Gulf War I deployment, there were increased rates of birth defects, miscarriages, infertility and genitourinary morbidity. In particular the incidence of Goldenhaar syndrome (GHS) captured public interest. However, Araneta *et al.* (1997) studied the incidence of GHS among 34 069 Gulf War veterans' infants and those of 41 345 non-deployment veterans, and found five and two cases in the groups, respectively. They concluded, given the very few cases found and the broad confidence limits of their analysis, that the results be treated with caution and did not exclude chance as an explanation for their findings.

Penman *et al.* (1996) reported that they had not found any evidence of an increase in birth defects or any special health problems amongst children of Persian Gulf War veterans in Mississippi. In a very large study, Cowan *et al.* (1997) investigated the risk of birth defects among children of Gulf War veterans, in which they analysed records of 33 998 infants born to Gulf War veterans, and 41 463 infants born to non-deployed veterans. This careful analysis did not reveal any evidence for an increased risk of birth defects among children of Gulf War veterans.

Araneta *et al.* (2003) published the results of their exhaustive study on birth defects among the children of Gulf War veterans. They analysed the prevalence of birth defects among the offspring of 684 645 Gulf War veterans (GWV) compared with 1 587 102 non-deployed veterans (NDV). They found 11 961 GWV infants and 33 052 NDV infants. They observed a higher prevalence of tricuspid valve insufficiency, aortic valve stenosis and renal hypoplasia among infants conceived post war to GWV and a higher prevalence of hypospadias among infants conceived post war to female GWV. However, they added the important caveat that this study could not determine whether any excess could be attributed to inherited or environmental factors, or was due to pure chance for a multitude of reasons, including multiple comparisons.

Doyle *et al.* (2004) published the results of their study on a very large number of Gulf veterans based on a questionnaire, addressing the issues of miscarriage, stillbirth and congenital malformations. From this analysis, covering 27 959 pregnancies reported by men and 861 pregnancies reported by women, all conceptions after first Gulf War, they concluded that there was no evidence for increased risk of stillbirth, chromosomal abnormalities or congenital syndromes. There is only one report of increased birth defects amongst offspring of Gulf War veterans (Kang *et al.*, 2001), but their methodology has been seriously questioned and the validity of their findings remains controversial.

In another study, by Maconochie *et al.* (2004), the issue of infertility among UK male Gulf War veterans was examined. They found a small increase of self-reported infertility but could not associate this finding with service in Gulf War 1. The results of this study were mirrored in the Danish study of male veterans who served in the Gulf between August 1990 and December 1997 (Ishoy *et al.*, 2001). The investigation looked at 661 male subjects who deployed compared to 215 who did not. The conclusion from this analysis was that the biological reproductive health of Danish Gulf War veterans appeared unaffected by their engagement in the post war peacekeeping mission. Bale and Lee (2005) found only

16 cases of oligospermia/infertility amongst 3233 Gulf veterans. This was not considered an exceptional finding.

Following Op Telic (Gulf War II, 2003), there were media reports of 'stillbirth and/or congenital abnormalities' (*Portsmouth Evening News* and national press, 2004) as a result of anthrax vaccinations. Not only were these allegations never confirmed by careful investigation, but also the Health Protection Agency (National Organisation for England and Wales) stated categorically 'There is no scientifically plausible basis to support a claim that a baby could be harmed by an inactivated (non-live) vaccine such as anthrax'. Once again the effect of irresponsible, non-researched media coverage could be seen as a cause of distress amongst veterans.

Male Gulf veterans reported a higher proportion of offspring with any type of malformation, but in particular some evidence of increased risk of malformations of the genital system, renal tract and 'other' defects of the digestive and musculoskeletal systems and non-chromosomal anomalies. However, the author counselled a very cautious interpretation of these findings and noted any associations were considerably weakened when analyses were restricted to clinically confirmed conditions as opposed to self-report. Among female Gulf veterans, no association was found between miscarriage and Gulf service.

From all the evidence available, the inevitable verdict must be that service in Gulf War I has not resulted in harm to reproductive health. Sadly, however, it is well known that some veterans, based on ill-informed, sensationalist media reports about congenital abnormalities in children of Gulf War veterans, decided against having children: a good example of the direct negative influence of false media reporting on veterans and their families! Perhaps it is worth noting that 38 % of all conceptions end in miscarriage and there is a 5 % incidence of any birth defect in all conceptions.

## MORTALITY STUDIES

Here again, there have been repeated claims by veterans' activist groups of increased mortality amongst Gulf War veterans. However, the comprehensive studies by Macfarlane *et al.* (2000), Kang and Bullman (2001) and the ongoing 6-monthly updates by DASA (2005, 2006) have not shown any increased mortality rates as a result of organic disease amongst Gulf War veterans. The recent Canadian study (2005) has not found any differences in mortality rates between deployed and non-deployed veterans.

## GENERAL OUTCOMES

An analysis of the larger surveys (US, France, UK, Canada, Australia) of post-Gulf War health outcomes allows some general and convincing observations to be made.

In 2002, the departments of Veterans Affairs published the clinical findings of 100 339 Gulf War veterans. This was a follow-up to that published by Joseph (1997). This comprehensive analysis was therefore based on detailed systematic clinical examinations on a cohort representing 14 % of all US forces deployed to the Gulf in 1990–91. It was also stressed that there is no substitute for actually examining ill patients, as opposed to questionnaires, if one is looking for a new syndrome or attempting to design research studies to answer a particular health issue. Like GVMAP, it is a self-referral programme without a control group, but given the large proportion of veterans seen over an 8-year period, this observational study allows further comment on veterans' health status similar to the observations made by Bale and Lee (2005) on UK veterans. However, no-one denies that caution must be exercised with the interpretation of non-controlled registry data, where self-selected participants may not be representative of the overall Gulf veteran population.

Although the US study could not determine whether or not there was a higher incidence of neurological, psychological, nephrological or neurological disorders among veterans, nevertheless they did not find that severely ill participants presented with a particular disease that could be associated with any specific wartime exposure. Neither did they find any evidence of an unusual syndrome, nor any predominant single type of illness. Another important compelling observation in this report was that no unique Gulf War syndrome/illness has yet been identified, either among military veterans from 40 other coalition forces (large and small) or amongst almost one million inhabitants of northern Saudi Arabia or Kuwait. As in the UK (Lee et al., 2002; Bale and Lee, 2005), so the American report underscores the fact that for veterans with well-known health problems (ICD-10 classification), or even with ICD-10 Chapter 18 diagnoses, there are well-tried effective treatments available.

The French have also published a study on Gulf Veteran health outcomes (Salamon, 2004). This involved sending a questionnaire to

10 476 veterans who could be located 10 years after the Gulf War out of 20 261 Service personnel who deployed. Of these, 5702 (28 %) responded, and for some this led to further clinical evaluation. Amongst army veterans (2695), the most commonly reported illnesses were osteoarticular complaints (422 ; 16 %), respiratory disorders (362; 13%) and eye conditions. During the actual conflict, 1278 (47 %) complained of diarrhoea, no doubt a variant of traveller's diarrhoea. Nevertheless, at the time of response, 2225 (83 %) stated they were in good or very good health. Of French naval Gulf veterans, 700 (43 %) responded out of a total of 1787 contacted. The most common post-Gulf diseases complained of were respiratory 86 (11 %), ophthalmic complaints 86 (11 %), and musculoskeletal disorders 75 (10 %). As with army veterans, the most common complaint during deployment was diarrhoea 171 (22 %). Most Naval veterans 727 (96 %) reported they were in good or very good health. Finally, of 1895 French Air Force personnel who responded, the most common complaints during deployment were diarrhoea 491 (26 %) and sleep disturbances. Post-conflict health concerns were respiratory 278 (15 %), musculoskeletal complaints 220 (12 %), eye disorders 214 (11 %), and digestive tract problems 203 (11 %). Nevertheless, at the time of response the majority in this group, 1678 (92 %), felt in good or very good health. Thus, overall, for the three services, 90.3 % claimed to be in good health. This compares very favourably with 75 % who were in good health in the UK series (Lee *et al.*, 2002).

As the authors of the French report emphasised, claims of exposures 10 years after the event are probably tainted by potential recall bias, which might in turn be influenced by health problems. Equally, they suggested that the disorders studied were mainly those reported by participants and could also be subject to recall bias. This mirrors precisely the MRC 2003 report, which found that Gulf veterans who report more severe symptoms are more likely to recall having had more vaccinations or exposures to insecticides/pesticides, but their perception of their health status, if poor, is known to induce recall bias. They found no evidence to support the concept of a 'Gulf War Syndrome' or any unique Gulf related disorder. Furthermore, the Salamon study did not reveal any unusual disorders and, in particular, did not find an unusual incidence of malignancies, haematological disorders, autoimmune complaints, or neurological disorders such as multiple sclerosis or amyotrophic lateral sclerosis. Psychological problems were frequently encountered.

A report on health outcomes for Canadian Gulf War veterans was published by Gilroy (1998). About 5100 Canadian personnel were deployed to the Gulf, of whom 2200 were there during the actual conflict. The study compared 5117 deployed with 6093 non-deployed. Deployed veterans had a higher prevalence of self-reported illnesses such as musculoskeletal disorders, digestive tract problems and skin and respiratory disorders, and also higher rates of depression, post-traumatic stress disorder and anxiety compared with non-deployed veterans. However, a distinctive syndrome or unique illness related to Gulf service did not emerge. Furthermore, this study did not show any consistent association between self-reported illness and exposures to substances or variable environmental conditions. This survey, therefore, reflects the health outcomes of veterans studied in other countries. Furthermore, a later study (Canadian Persian Gulf Cohort Study, 2005) did not reveal any differences in cancer or mortality rates between deployed and non-deployed veterans.

The UK GVMAP studies showed similar outcomes to those reported above. Although Hull *et al.* (2002) suggested that Gulf veterans attending GVMAP were not representative of Gulf veterans as a whole; nevertheless this conclusion was based on a sample of only 173 veterans who had attended their institute and GVMAP. The reports by Lee *et al.* (2002) and Bale and Lee (2005) were based on 3000 and 3233 veterans respectively. These studies did not support veterans' activist groups who claimed increased incidences of infertility, birth defects, pregnancy problems, rheumatological, nephrological, neurological and immunological disorders and unusual cancers amongst veterans. Nor were any unusual disease trends noted between 1993–2004. The majority were well in keeping with the observation by Unwin *et al.* (1999) that, although veterans reported more symptoms, their physical functional capacity (SP36) was not compromised.

Perhaps the most striking difference between the US studies and those of other nationalities was that they found that only between 6–9 % of veterans were well, whereas other reports found that more than 75 % were well. This may reflect different health seeking strategies in the US where there is no form of free healthcare.

## CONCLUSION

From all these studies, many of which have been longitudinal, based on large numbers evaluated and not relying only on questionnaires, a number of conclusions can be drawn.

There is no evidence to support the concept of a new disorder such as 'Gulf War Syndrome'. It is time to abandon this hypothesis to prevent further large sums of money being spent on fruitless research and thereby help veterans to focus on real illnesses for which there are treatments. The label of 'Gulf War Syndrome' does not help a veteran get special treatment.

All the evidence shows that over the past decade, no unusual disease patterns have emerged and no particular human system has been particularly compromised as a result of Gulf service. Many Gulf veterans report a similar array of nondescript symptoms as the general population. Mortality rates as a result of physical disease are not higher amongst veterans compared with the general population or era groups. There is an undeniable psychiatric cost to war and addressing such problems as soon as possible after returning from a conflict deployment is the best way to help veterans. Also, a closer interaction between the medical profession and the media and politicians could well help defuse the large amount of misinformation that appears in the media, which of itself causes considerable distress to veterans.

# REFERENCES

Amato, A. A., McVey, A., Cha, C., Matthews, E. C., Jackson, C. E., Kleingunther, R., Worley, L., Cornman, E. and Kagan-Hallet K. (1997). Evaluation of neuromuscular symptoms in veterans of the Persian Gulf War, *Neurol.*, **48**, 4–12.

Araneta, M. R. G., Destiche, D. A., Schlangen, K. M., Merz, R. D., Forrester, M. B. and Gray, G. C. (2000). Birth defects prevalence among infants of Persian Gulf War veterans born in Hawaii, *Teratology*, **62**, 195–204.

Araneta, M. R. G., Moore, C. A., Olney, R. S., Edmond, S. L. D., Marcher, J. A., McDonough, C., Hillopoulos, K. M., Schlangen, K. M. and Gray, G. C. (1997). Goldenhar Syndrome among infants born in military hospitals to Gulf War veterans. *Teratology*, **56**, 244–51.

Araneta, M. R. G., Schlangen, K. M., Edmonds, L. D., Destiche, D. A., Merz, R. D., Hobbs, C. A., Flood, T. J., Harris, J. A., Krishnamvarti, D. and Gray, G. C. (2003). Prevalence of birth defects among infants of Gulf War veterans in Arkansas, Arizona, California, Georgia, Hawaii and Iowa 1989–93, *Birth Defects Research* (Part A), **67**, 246–60.

Bale, A. J. and Lee, H. A. (2005). An observational study on diagnoses of 3233 Gulf veterans (Op Granby 299091) who attended the Ministry of Defence's Medical Assessment Programme 1993–2004, *J. Royal Naval Medical Service*, **91**, 99–111.

Beghi, E. and Morrison, K. E. (2005). ALS and military service, *Neurology*, **64**, 6–7.

Binder, L. M. and Campbell, K. A. (2004). Medically unexplained symptoms and neuropsychological assessment, *J. Clin. Exper. Neuropsych.*, **26**, 369–92.

Blatchley, N. F. W., Lee, H. A. and Bolton, J. P. G. (2003). Reduced bone formation in UK Gulf War veterans: a bone histomorphometric study, *J. Clin. Pathol.*, **56**, 559.

Briggs, J. (1995). The tiny victims of Desert Storm, *Life* (Nov.), 46–61.

Canadian Persian Gulf Cohort Study (2005). *Summary report*, Client Services, Health Statistics Division, Statistics, Canada, Ottawa, Ontario. www.statcan.ca

Carson, A. J. *et al.* (2003). *J. Neurol. Neurosurg. Psychiat.*, **74**, 897–900.

Cherry, N., Creed, F., Silman, A., Dunn, G., Baxter, D., Smedley, J., Taylor, S. and Macfarlane, G. J. (2001). Health and exposures of United Kingdom Gulf War veterans. Part II: The relation of health to exposure, *Occup. Environ. Med.*, **58**, 299–306.

Clase, M. C., Garg, A. X. and Kiberd, B. A. (2004). Classifying kidney problems: can we avoid framing risks as diseases? *British Medical Journal*, **329**, 912–15.

Colwill, J. M. (Ed.) (2003). *Gulf War and Health*, Vol 2. *Insecticides and Solvents*, Washington, DC: National Academies Press.

Combined Analysis of the VA and DoD Gulf War Clinical Evaluation Programs (2002). *A Study of the Clinical Findings from Systematic Medical Examinations of 100 339 US Gulf War Veterans*, Department of Veterans Affairs, Veterans Health Administration and Department of Defense, Office of the Assistant Secretary of Defense, Health Affairs, Washington, DC.

Compston, J. E., Vedi, S., Stephen, A. B., Bord, S., Lyons, A. R., Hodges, S. J. and Scammell, J. (2002). Reduced bone formation in UK Gulf War veterans, *J. Clin. Pathol.*, **55**, 897–99.

Cowan, D. N., Defraitas, R. F., Gray, G. C., Goldenbaum, M. B. and Wishik, S. M. (1997). The risk of birth defects among children of Persian Gulf War veterans, *New England Journal of Medicine*, **336**, 1650–56.

Defence Analytical Services Agency (DASA) (2005). http://www.dasa.mod.uk/natstats/gulf/ntr.html.

DASA Defence Analytical Services Agency (DASA) (2006). http://www.dasa.mod.uk/natstats/gulf/ntr.html.

David, A. S., Farrin, L., Hull, L., Unwin, C., Wessely, S. and Wykes, T. (2002). Cognitive functioning and disturbance of mood in UK veterans of the Persian Gulf War: a comparative study, *Psychol. Med.*, **32**, 1327–70.

Davis, L. E., Eisen, S. A., Murphy, F. M., Alpern, R., Parks, B. J., Blanchard, M., Reda, D. J., King, M. K., Mithen, F. A. and Kang, H. K. (2004). Clinical and laboratory assessment of distal peripheral nerves in Gulf War veterans and spouses, *Neurology*, **63**, 1070–77.

Department of Veterans' Affairs (2002).

Doebbeling, B. N., Clarke, W. R., Watson, D., Torner, J. C., Woolson, R. F., Voelker, M. D. and Barrett, D. H. (2000). Reply to R. W/ Haley's letter, *American Journal of Medicine*, **109**, 745–47.

Doyle, P., Maconochie, N., Davies, G., Maconochie, I., Pelerin, M., Prior, S. and Lewis, S. (2004). Miscarriage, stillbirth and congenital malformation in the offspring of veterans of the first Gulf War, *International Journal of Epidemiology*, **33**, 74–86.

Eisen, S. A., Kang, H. K., Murphy, F. M., Clanchard, M. S., Reda, D. J., Henderson, W. G., Toomey, R., Jackson, L. W., Alpern, R. *et al.* (2005). Gulf War veterans' health: medical evaluation of a US cohort, *Annals of Internal Medicine*, **142**, 881–90.

England, J. D. and Asprey, A. K. (2004). Peripheral neuropathy, *Lancet*; **363**, 2151–61.

Ferrari, R. and Russell , A. S. (2001). The problem of Gulf War Syndrome, *Med. Hypoth.*, **56**, 697–701.

Forbes, A. B., McKenzie, D. P., MacKinnon, A. J., Kelsall, H. L., McFarlane, A. C., Ikin, J. F., Glass, D. C. and Sim, M. R. (2004). The health of Australian veterans of the

1991 Gulf War: factor analysis of self-reported symptoms, *Occup. Environ. Med.*, **61**, 1014–20.

Freemont, A. J. (2002). Bone and the Gulf War: osteoblastis – possible victims of the Gulf War? *Journal of Clinical Pathology*, **55**, 884.

Fulco, C. E., Liverman, C. T. and Sox, H. C. (2000). *Gulf War and Health*, Vol 1. *Depleted Uranium, Pyridostigmine Bromide, Sarin, Vaccines*, Washington, DC: National Academies Press.

Gilroy, G. (1998). *Health Study of Canadian Forces Personnel Involved in the 1991 Conflict in the Persian Gulf*, Ottawa, Ontario: Department of National Defence (DND).

Gray, G. C., Coate, B. D., Anderson, C. M., Kang, H. K., Berg, S. W., Wignall, F. S., Knoke, J. D. and Barrett-Connor E. (1996). The post war hospitalization experience of US veterans in the Persian Gulf War, *New England Journal of Medicine*, **335**, 1498–504.

Greenberg, N., Wessely, S., Iversen, A., Hull, L., Unwin, C. and Destrange, M. (2003). Vaccination records in Gulf War veterans, *J Occup. Environ. Med.*, **45**, 219–21.

Haley, R. W. (2000). Will we solve the Gulf War Syndrome puzzle by population surveys or clinical research? (letter), *American Journal of Medicine*, **109**, 744–45.

Haley, R. W. (2003). Excess incidence of ALS in young Gulf War veterans, *Neurology*, **61**, 650–56.

Haley, R. W. and Kurt, T. L. (1997). Self-reported exposure to neurotoxic chemical combinations in the Gulf War: a cross-sectional study, *Journal of the American Medical Association*, **277**, 231–37.

Haley, R. W., Thomas, K. L. and Horn, J. (1997a). Is there a Gulf War syndrome? Searching for syndromes by factor analysis of symptoms, *Journal of the American Medical Association*, **277**, 215–22.

Haley, R. W., Horn, J., Roland, P. S., *et al.* (1997b). Evaluation of neurologic function in Gulf War veterans: a blinded case control study, *Journal of the American Medical Association*, **277**, 223–30.

Haley, R. W., Marshall, W. W., MacDonald, G. G., Dougherty, M. A., Petty, F. and Fleckenstein, J. L. (2000a). Brain abnormalities in Gulf War Syndrome: evaluation with 1H HMR spectroscopy, *Radiology*, **215**, 807–17.

Haley, R. W., Fleckenstein, J. L., Marshall, W. W., *et al.* (2000b). Effect of basal ganglia injury on central dopamine activity in Gulf War Syndrome: correlation of MR spectroscopy and plasma homovanillic acid, *Arch. Neurol.*, **57**, 1280–85.

Haley, R. W., Vongpatanasin, W., Wolfe, G. I., *et al.* (2004). Blunted circadian variation in autonomic regulation of sinus node function in veterans with Gulf War syndrome, *American Journal of Medicine*, **117**, 469–78.

Hansard (2005). *Gulf Veterans' Illnesses*, 13 June; IWS.

Health Protection Agency (Centre for Infections) (2005). London: webteam@hpa.org.uk

Higgins, E. M., Ismail, K., Kant, K., Harman, K., Mellerio, J., Du Vivier, A. W. P. and Wessely, S. (2002). Skin disease in Gulf War veterans, *Quarterly Journal of Medicine*, **95**, 671–76.

Horner, R. D., Kamins, K. G., Feussner, J. R., *et al.* (2003). Occurrence of amyotrophic lateral sclerosis among Gulf War veterans, *Neurology*, **61**, 742–49.

Hotopf, M., David, A., Hull, L., Ismail, K., Unwin, C. and Wessely, S. (2000). Role of vaccinations as risk factors for ill-health in veterans of the Gulf War: cross-sectional study, *British Medical Journal*, **320**, 1363–67.

Hull, L., David, A. S., Hyams, K. C., Unwin, C., Wessely, S. C. and Hotopf, M. (2002). Self-reported health of Persian Gulf War veterans: a comparison of help-seeking and randomly ascertained cases, *Military Medicine*, **167**, 747–52.

Institute of Medicine USA (2001).

Ishoy, T., Andersson, A.-M., Suadicani, P., Guldager, B., Appleyard, M., Gyhntelberg, F. and Skakkeboek, N. E. (2001). Major reproductive health characteristics in male Gulf War veterans, *Danish Medical Bulletin*, **48**, 28–32.

Ismail, K., Everitt, B., Blatchley, N., Hull, L., Unwin, C., David, A. and Wessely, S. (1999). Is there a Gulf War Syndrome? *Lancet*, **353**, 179–82.

Jerome, R., Breu, G. and McKenna, K. (1995). An enemy within, *People*, Jan., 32–7.

Jones, E. and Wessely, S. (2005). Hearts, guts and minds: somatisation in the military from 1900, *Journal of Psychosomatic Research*, **56**, 425–29.

Joseph, S. C. (1997). A comprehensive clinical evaluation of 20 000 Persian Gulf War veterans, *Military Medicine*, **162**, 149–55.

Joseph, T. K., Foster, L. and Pasquina, P. F. (2004). Decreased prevalence of peripheral nerve pathology by electrodiagnostic testing in Gulf War veterans, *Military Medicine*, **11**, 868–72.

Kang, H. K. and Bullman, T. (1996). Mortality amongst US veterans of the Persian Gulf War, *New England Journal of Medicine*, **335**, 1498–1504.

Kang, H. K. and Bullman, T. (2001). Mortality among US veterans of Persian Gulf War: 7-year follow-up, *American Journal of Epidemiology*, **154**, 399–405.

Kang, H. K., Mahan, C. M., Lee, K. Y., Magee, C. A. and Murphy, F. M. (2000). Illnesses among United States veterans of the Gulf War: a population-based survey of 30 000 veterans, *J. Occup. Environ. Med.*, **42**, 491–501.

Kang, H. K., Magee, C., Mahan, C., Lee, K., Murphy, F., Jackson, L. and Matanoski, G. (2001). Pregnancy outcomes among US Gulf War veterans: a population-based survey of 30 000 veterans, *Ann. Epidemiol.*, **11**, 504–11.

Karlinsky, J. B., Blanchard, M., Alpern, R., Eisen, S. A., Kang, H., Murphy, F. M. and Reda, D. J. (2004). Late prevalence of respiratory symptoms and pulmonary function abnormalities in Gulf War I veterans, *Arch. Intern. Med.*, **164**, 2488–91.

Kelsall, H. L., Sim, M. R., Forbes, A. B., Glass, D. C., McKenzie, D. P., Ikin, J. F., Abramson, M. J., Blizzard, L. and Ittak, P. (2004). Symptoms and medical conditions in Australian veterans of the 1991 Gulf War: relation to immunizations and other Gulf War exposures, *Occup. Environ. Med.*, **61**, 1006–13.

Kelsall, H. L., MacDonell, R., Sim, M., Forbes, A., McKenzie, D., Glass, D., Ikin, J. and Ittak, P. (2005). Neurological status of Australian veterans of the 1991 Gulf War and the effect of medical and chemical exposures, *International Journal of Epidemiology*, 841–49.

Komatroff, A. I. (2005). Unexplained suffering in the aftermath of war, *Annals of Internal Medicine*, **142**, 938–39.

Landragran, P. (1997). Illness in Gulf War veterans: causes and consequences, *Journal of the American Medical Association*,; **277**, 259–61.

Lee, H. A., Gabriel, R. and Bale, A. J. (2002). Health status and clinical diagnoses of 3000 UK Gulf War veterans, *Journal of the Royal Society of Medicine*, **95**, 491–97.

Lee, H. A., Bale, A. J. and Gabriel, R. (2005). Results of investigations on Gulf War veterans, *Clinical Medicine*, **5**, 166–72.

Leigh, N. (2002). *Incidence of motor neurone disease*, personal communication.

Lewis, T. (1944). Reflections upon medical education, *Lancet*, i, 619–21.

Macfarlane, G. J., Thomas, E. and Cherry, N. (2000). Mortality amongst UK Gulf War veterans, *Lancet*, **356**, 17–21.

Maconochie, N., Doyle, P. and Carson, C. (2004). Infertility among male UK veterans of the 1990–1 Gulf War: reproductive cohort study. *British Medical Journal*, doi: 10.1136/bmj.38163.620972. AE (published 14 July).

Medical Research Council (2003). *Review of Research into UK Gulf Veterans Illnesses*, London: MRC.

Menon, P. M., Nasrallah, H. A., Reeves, R. R. and Jeffrey, A. (2004). Hippocampal dysfunction in Gulf War Syndrome. A proton MR spectroscopy study, *Brain Research*, **1009**, 189–94.

Milner, B. I., Kozol, R., Khuri, S., Hur, Q. and Fligiel, W. E. G. (1998). Gallbladder disease in Gulf War veterans. Conference of Federally Sponsored Gulf War Veterans' Illness Research, 17–19 June, Washington, DC.

Murphy, F. M. (1999). Gulf War Syndrome. There may be no specific syndrome but troops suffer after most wars, *British Medical Journal*, **318**, 274–75.

Newmark, J. and Clayton, W. L. (1995). Persian Gulf illnesses: preliminary neurological impressions, *Military Medicine*, **160**, 505–7.

Peakman, M., Skowera, A. and Hotopf, M. (2006). Immunological dysfunction, vaccination and Gulf War illness, *Philosophical Transactions of the Royal Society B*, **361**, 681–87.

Penman, A. D., Currier, M. M. and Tarver, R. S. (1996). No evidence of increase in birth defects and health problems among children of Gulf War veterans, *Military Medicine*, **161**, 1–6.

*Portsmouth Evening News* (2004).

Quiner, J. L. and Coan, M. L. (1999). Fibromyalgia falls foul of fallacy. *Lancet*, **353**, 1092–94.

River-Zayas, J., Arroyo, M. and Mejias, E. (2001). Evaluation of Persian Gulf veterans with symptoms of peripheral neuropathy, *Military Medicine*, **166**, 449–552.

Rook, G. A. W. and Zumla, A. (1997). Gulf War Syndrome: is it due to a systemic shift in cytokine balance towards a Th2 profile? Lancet, **39**, 1831–33.

Rose, M. R. and Brix, K. A. (2006). Neurological disorders in Gulf War veterans, *Philosophical Transactions of the Royal Society B*, **361**, 605–18.

Rosof, B. M. and Hernandez, L. M. (Eds). (2001). *Gulf War Veterans: Treating Symptoms and Syndromes*, Washington DC: National Academy Press, .

Salamon, R. (2004). *The French Study on the Gulf War and its Impact on Health*, INSERM U593 (formerly U330), 33076 Bordeaux Cedex.

Sharief, M. K., Priddin, J., Delamont, R. S., Unwin, C., Rose, M. R., David, A. and Wessely, S. (2002). Neurophysiologic analysis of neuromuscular symptoms in UK Gulf War veterans, *Neurology*, **59**, 1518–25.

Smith, T. C., Gray, G. C. and Knoke, J. D. (2000). Is systemic lupus erythematosus, amyotrophic lateral sclerosis or fibromyalgia associated with Persian Gulf War service. An examination of Department of Defense Hospitalization Data, *American Journal of Epidemiology*, **151**, 53–8.

Southwick, S. M., Morgan, C. A., Nicolaou, A. L. and Charney, D. S. (1997). Consistency of memory for combat-related traumatic events in veterans of Operation Desert Storm, *American Journal of Psychiatry*, **154**, 173–77.

Storzbach, D., Rohlman, D. S., Anger, W. K., Binder, L. M., Campbell, K. and members of the Portland Environmental Hazards Research Center. (2001). Neurobehavioural deficits in Persian Gulf War veterans: additional evidence from a population-based study, *Environmental Research*, **85**, 1–13.

Svensson, A. L., Suadicani, P., Guldager, B., Ishoy, T., Appleyard, M. and Gyntelberg, F. (2000). Self-reported dyspnoea is strongly associated with psychological and cognitive symptoms, *Ugeskr. Laeger*, **162**, 687–91.

Tipit, S. (1994). What's wrong with our children? *Ladies Home Journal*, June, 100–48.

Unwin, C., Blatchley, N., Coker, W. J., Ferry, S., Hotopf, M., Hull, L., *et al.* (1999). The health of United Kingdom Servicemen who served in the Persian Gulf War, *Lancet*, **353**, 169–78.

Vasterling, J. J. and Bremner, J. D. (2006). The impact of the 1991 Gulf War on the mind and brain: findings from neuropsychological and neuroimaging research, *Philosophical Transactions of the Royal Society B*, **361**, 593–604.

Weisskopf, M. G., O'Reilly. E. J., McCullough, M. L. *et al.* (2004). Prospective study of military service and mortality from amyotrophic lateral sclerosis, *Neurology*, **64**,32–7.

World Health Organisation (1992). *ICD-10: International Statistical Classification of Diseases and Related Health Problems*, tenth revision, Vol. 1, Geneva: WHO.

# 7

# Conclusion

Harry Lee and Edgar Jones

During the latter part of the Twentieth century, few medical issues have caused more controversy than the nature of so-called 'Gulf War syndrome'. Since it was first described in 1993, two years after the conflict had ended, it has been a source of acrimonious debate. Disaffected veterans and their supporters, recruited from science, politics and the media, drew battle lines against groups of medical researchers, who were often depicted as being in league with government. In essence, veterans reported a range of common symptoms for which no obvious medical explanation could be found. In addition, there were more worrying reports of birth defects in children born to Gulf ex-servicemen, and often a link was made between any veteran who died as a result of disease and his earlier deployment to the Middle East. As the debate unfolded, a bewildering variety of causal hypotheses were proposed: multiple vaccines, smoke inhalation from oil-well fires, organophosphates sprayed to kill insects, the fall-out from chemical weapons and the effects of DU munitions. A common theme in all these explanations was the toxic effect of an external agent.

The first point to make is that the term 'Gulf War Syndrome' has no scientific validity as no new illness or symptom cluster unique to Gulf War veterans has been identified (Unwin *et al.*, 1999; Ismail *et al.*, 1999; Cherry *et al.*, 2001; Shapiro *et al.*, 2002; Knoke *et al.*, 2000; Lee *et al.*, 2002). It is, however, appropriate to refer to 'Gulf War related illness', or even a 'Gulf War health effect', which is a cultural as

*War and Health: Lessons from the Gulf War*   Edited by Harry Lee & Edgar Jones
© 2007 John Wiley & Sons, Ltd

much as a medical phenomenon. Furthermore, the incidence of virtually all well-defined illnesses and diseases is not elevated in Gulf War veterans.

If there was nothing further to be observed about the phenomenon of 'Gulf War syndrome', then it would probably have drifted into obscurity. Yet it is incontrovertible that rates of 'ill health' (in essence self-reported illnesses) are greater in Gulf War veterans than in members of the armed forces who did not deploy (Unwin *et al.*, 1999; Fukuda *et al.*, 1998; Cherry *et al.*, 2001; Gray *et al.*, 2002; Iowa Persian Gulf Study Group, 1997). This finding applies to servicemen from the US, Canada, UK and Australia. Typically, symptoms reported by veterans include chronic fatigue, pain and cognitive impairment. However, the term 'ill health' requires careful definition and should not be confused with disease. The US Department of Defense refers to these symptom clusters as 'Gulf War veterans' illnesses' because they do not represent a unique illness as implied by 'Gulf War syndrome' (Donta *et al.*, 2003). In the US, Gulf War veterans are more likely to be admitted to hospital than are appropriately chosen controls, but the increased risk is for mental health diagnoses, multi-symptom conditions, and musculoskeletal disorders. If the distinction drawn by Kleinman (1988) and others between disease (for which there is pathological evidence of dysfunction) and illness (in which a person reports symptomatic distress and suffering but no pathological condition can be found) is accepted, then at the moment some Gulf veterans are suffering from illness, but not disease. So far there has been no evidence of an increase in mortality in Gulf veterans from the United States or the United Kingdom, with the exception of deaths from suicide and accidents (Macfarlane *et al.*, 2000; Kang and Bullman, 2001).

How then can we explain the phenomenon of 'Gulf War syndrome'? First, following a rapid victory and no untoward medical problems in the field, governments in the US and UK were caught by surprise. Military physicians were also unprepared for the epidemic of claims and assertions. No one had a clear strategy for how to respond to the controversy which, having attracted the attention of the media and other interested parties, developed a momentum of its own. In the UK, the government made the cardinal error of dismissing the claims without acknowledging that they were potentially serious and could be resolved only by serious scientific investigation. This was a flawed response not least because without pre-deployment health screening, the government was unable to state categorically that returning veterans had not suffered adverse effects while in the Middle East. Not until December 1996 were studies into the health effects of the Gulf War commissioned in the UK (Cherry *et al.*, 2001; Doyle *et al.*, 2004). Indeed, not until the following year were scientific studies published in the US that began to address the long-term health effects of deployment to Iraq, Kuwait and Saudi Arabia (David *et al.*, 1997).

This delay had many adverse consequences (Hotopf and Wessely, 2005). An opportunity to research any chain of causation was lost. Did symptoms arise in the US and UK simultaneously (suggesting a common origin in the direct effects of war) or was there a time lag (suggesting indirect effects related to culture and the impact of the media). Turnover in the UK armed forces is high (around 5 % leaving every year). Hence by 1996 a sizeable minority of Gulf veterans had been discharged from the army, creating major difficulties in testing their health status. Although a wide range of studies has failed to identify a unique disorder related to the Gulf, there are exceptions to this pattern. These conflicting results may also be the product of the significant delay between veterans reporting symptoms and the implementation of programmes for their scientific investigation. For example, some abnormal findings may relate to events that have occurred after the war but that have been misinterpreted as a direct consequence of toxic exposures. In general, research into so-called Gulf War syndrome has been hampered by low response rates, ascertainment bias (the fact that response rates tend to be higher in Gulf veterans than control groups), recall bias, difficulties identifying suitable control groups (we have argued that the soldiers' experience of having to risk their lives on a routine basis is virtually unique), and problems defining the outcomes to study, given that most veterans present with multiple symptoms but few clear diagnoses (Hotopf and Wessely, 2005).

The delay in commissioning scientific studies created fertile ground for wild hypotheses, fuelled by the Internet, conspiracy theories and media speculation. Whenever a Gulf veteran died, from whatever cause, the local press would attribute their death to their war service without any other explanation or denominator data. Speculation grew in the absence of hard evidence. The cover of *Life* magazine for 1 November 1995, for example, under the headline 'The tiny victims of Desert Storm' depicted a US veteran of the Gulf in uniform standing next to his young son who had an obvious and distressing birth defect. It was hardly surprising that veterans became increasingly concerned, particularly in view of the serious charges being raised – that children born to Gulf veterans were at greater risk of stillbirth and that ex-servicemen themselves were experiencing elevated rates of cancer. In 1996, the National Gulf Veterans and

Families Association (NGVFA) was founded and shortly after produced their booklet *What is Gulf War Illness?* In this publication, the group speculated, on the basis of anecdotal observations, about the causes of Gulf veterans' ill health. Regrettably, their suppositions were latched on to by some politicians and sections of the media. The NGVFA, though well meaning, may have caused distress among Gulf War veterans by publicising claims not supported by objective medical evidence. In this environment of uncertainty and rumour, 'convictions', observed the German philosopher Nietzsche (1878, p. 483), 'are more dangerous enemies of the truth than lies'.

Whilst most of the 53 000 UK troops deployed to the Middle East managed the difficult transition from war to peace successfully, a vocal and motivated minority suggested that their long-term health might have been damaged by non-combat aspects of military service in the Gulf. In November 1994, amid stories of a cover-up and before scientific studies had been commissioned by the government, a group of ex-servicemen formed themselves into the Gulf Veterans' Association (GVA) to campaign for a thorough investigation of the question. Later, the NGVFA, based in Hull, was set up by former members of the GVA. Hence, during a period of uncertainty, a number of pressure groups were formed with different aims, philosophies and varied memberships. In April 1998, in an attempt to draw them together, the British Legion set up a Gulf Veterans' branch based in Newcastle. It comprised representatives from the GVA, VetNet and the Middle East Forces Veterans' Association. However, the NGVFA refused to join, so there is no single voice representing veterans of the war. Indeed, one reason why the controversy has proved so lengthy and acrimonious was plausibly because of the factional interests involved.

Fifteen years after the end of the Gulf War, and following the expenditure of $200 million in the US (Deployment Health Working Group, 2003), and a further £8.5 million by the UK government (Caplin, 2005), there can be little justification for further research. If further sums were to be provided from national budgets, it would be more appropriate to target treatments, such as CBT programmes for servicemen with PTSD, or to explore other interventions that might effectively address these chronic disorders.

Whilst international research conducted across various disciplines has allowed us to state what Gulf War syndrome is not, some questions remain unanswered. Why did this particular conflict generate so many discontented veterans with health concerns and generate such strong beliefs? For a small group, as Kilshaw has argued, the label may provide a sense of meaning and a focus for self-support groups. Even if this is the case, it does not explain why no such phenomenon was observed after the Korean War (1950–53) and, to date, why no similar health concerns have been expressed following the deployment of British and US troops to Afghanistan and Iraq.

'Gulf War syndrome' has entered late-Twentieth century culture as surely as 'shell shock' cast a shadow across the interwar period. In 1998, for example, a study showed that 17 % of UK Gulf veterans believed they were suffering from 'Gulf War syndrome' (Chalder *et al.*, 2001), while 21 % of US Gulf veterans currently receive some form of disability support from the Veterans' Administration. At the time of writing, 10 % of UK Gulf War veterans are in receipt of either war pensions or gratuities. With the benefit of hindsight, had the medical authorities in the US and UK set up targeted random controlled trials in 1993, then any legitimate veteran questions could plausibly have been resolved before they had become inflamed by claims of conspiracy and cover-up. The principal lesson of the episode is that epidemiological and health studies should be planned before military action is contemplated and executed as soon as troops return from theatre. Accurate evidence gathered at the time prevents the growth of rumour, speculation, and any claim of malpractice.

There is now general agreement in medical parlance that 'Gulf War Syndrome' or any unique Gulf War illness does not exist (Wessely and Freedman, 2006). There is also consensus that deaths from organic disease, apart from post-traumatic injuries, are not increased amongst veterans (Gray and Kang, 2006). Many causation theories for Gulf War illnesses have appeared over the past 14 years, but none has been substantiated. We agree with Wessely and Freedman that further research into the aetiology of Gulf War illness will prove fruitless so long after the event. It is time to stop looking back and concentrate on the future, developing improved treatment strategies for Gulf veterans who remain ill.

# REFERENCES

Caplin, I. (2005). *House of Commons Official Report*, Cols. 236–7WH.

Chalder, T., Hotopf, M. and Hull, L., *et al.* (2001). Prevalence of Gulf war veterans who believe they have Gulf war syndrome: questionnaire study, *British Medical Journal*, **323**, 473–76.

Cherry, N., Creed, F., Silman, A., *et al.* (2001). Health and exposures of United Kingdom Gulf war veterans, Part 1: the pattern and extent of ill health, *Occupational and Environmental Medicine*, 58, 291–98.

David, A., Ferry, S. and Wessely, S. (1997). Gulf War illness, New American research provides leads but no firm conclusions, *British Medical Journal*, 314, 239–40.

Deployment Health Working Group Research Subcommittee (2005). *Annual Report to Congress: Federally Sponsored Research on Gulf War Veterans' Illnesses for 2003*, Washington DC: VA.

Donta, S.T., Clauw, D.J., Engel, C.C., Guarino, P., *et al.* (2003). Cognitive behavioural therapy and aerobic exercise for Gulf War veterans' illnesses: a randomised controlled trial, *Journal of the American Medical Association*, 289, 1396–404.

Doyle, P., Maconochie, N., Davies, G., Maconochie, I., Pelerin, M., Prior, S. and Lewis, S. (2004). Miscarriage, stillbirth and congenital malformation in the offspring of UK veterans of the first Gulf war, *International Journal of Epidemiology*, 33, 74–86.

Fukuda, K., Nisenbaum, R., Stewart, G. (1998). Chronic multisymptom illness affecting airforce veterans of the Gulf War, *Journal of the American Medical Association*, 289: 981–88.

Gray, G. C. and Kang, H. K. (2006). Healthcare utilization and mortality among veterans of the Gulf War, *Philosophical Transactions of the Royal Society B*, 361, 553–70.

Gray, G.C., Reed, R.J., Kaiser, K.S., Smith, T.C., Gastanaga, V.M. (2002). Self-reported symptoms and medical conditions among 11 868 Gulf War-era veterans: the Seebee health study, *American Journal of Epidemiology*, 155, 1033–44.

Hotopf, M. and Wessely, S. (2005). Can epidemiology clear the fog of war? Lessons from the 1990–91 Gulf War, *International Journal of Epidemiology*, 34, 791–800.

Iowa Persian Gulf Study Group (1997). Self reported illness and health status among Gulf War veterans: a population-based study, *Journal of the American Medical Association*, 277, 238–45.

Ismail, K., Everitt, B., Blatchley, N., *et al.* (1999). Is there a Gulf War syndrome? *Lancet*, 353, 179–82.

Kang, H.K. and Bullman, T.A. (2001). Mortality among US veterans of the Persian Gulf War: 7-year follow-up, *American Journal of Epidemiology*, 154, 399–405.

Kleinman, A. (1988). *Patients and Healers in The Context of Culture: An Exploration of the Borderland Between Anthropology, Medicine, and Psychiatry*, Berkeley: University of California Press.

Knoke, J.D., Smith, T.C., Gray, G.C., Kaiser, K.S. and Hawksworth, A.W. (2000). Factor analysis of self-reported symptoms: does it identify a Gulf War syndrome? *American Journal of Epidemiology*, 152, 379–88.

Lee, H.A., Gabriel, R., Bolton, J.P.G., Bale, A.J. and Jackson, M. (2002). Health status and clinical diagnoses of 3000 Gulf War veterans, *Journal of the Royal Society of Medicine*, 95, 491–97.

Lloyd, Lord, Jones, N. and Davies, M. (2004). *Independent Public Inquiry on Gulf War Illnesses*, London: Pattinson & Brewer.

Macfarlane, G.J., Thomas, E. and Cherry, N. (2000). Mortality among UK Gulf War veterans, *Lancet*, 356, 17–21.

National Gulf Veterans & Families Association (NGVFA) (1995). *What is Gulf War illness?* Copyright of NGVFA.

Nietzsche, F. (1878). *Human, All Too Human. Enemies of Truth*. London: Penguin Classics, 1994.

Shapiro, S.E., Lasarev, M.R. and McCauley, I. (2002). Factor analysis of Gulf War illness: what does it add to our understanding of possible health effects of deployment? *American Journal of Epidemiology*, **156**, 578–85.

Unwin, C., Blatchley, N., Coker, W., *et al.* (1999). The health of United Kingdom Servicemen who served in the Persian Gulf War, *Lancet*, **353**, 169–78.

Wessely, S. and Freedman, L. (2006). Reflections on Gulf War illness, *Philosophical Transactions of the Royal Society, B*, **361**, 721–30.

# Index

*Note*: Figures and Tables are indicated by *italic page numbers*; 'GWS' = 'Gulf War syndrome'

*War and Health: Lessons from the Gulf War*  Edited by Harry Lee & Edgar Jones
© 2007 John Wiley & Sons, Ltd